Insurance Dictionary

Also by Michael C. Thomsett

Insurance Dictionary

compiled by
Michael C. Thomsett

McFarland & Company, Inc., Publishers
Jefferson, North Carolina, and London

British Library Cataloguing-in-Publication data available

Library of Congress Cataloguing-in-Publication Data

Thomsett, Michael C.
 Insurance dictionary / by Michael C. Thomsett.
  p. cm.
 ISBN 0-89950-391-8 (lib. bdg.; 50# acid-free natural paper) ∞
 1. Insurance—Dictionaries. 2. Insurance—Abbreviations—
Dictionaries. I. Title.
HG151.T48 1989
368'.003'21—dc19   88-7947
                                                          CIP

Printed in the United States of America.

McFarland & Company, Inc., Publishers
 Box 611, Jefferson, North Carolina 28640

for my beneficiaries

Table of Contents

Introduction: What This Book Will Do for You

The *Insurance Dictionary* is a comprehensive summary of industry words and phrases and their meanings.

Insurance is an especially complex and confusing industry with its own terminology. The combination of investment, actuarial, legal and marketing phrases is difficult to master, even for professionals in the field.

The dictionary is divided into several sections:

Glossary of Terms. This largest section provides fully cross-referenced terms for insurance practices, theories and agencies. When appropriate, concepts are illustrated to facilitate explanations.

State Insurance Commissioner Addresses. This is a current listing of contact addresses for each state.

Canadian Provincial Agency Addresses. The current listing of contact addresses for each province in Canada is provided here.

Abbreviations. This section is an alphabetical summary of abbreviations, including terms, phrases, agencies and associations.

This book is a valuable reference for both the insurance professional and the consumer. It will help the reader to understand practices and theories of a wide range of insurance products, industry standards and practices.

Glossary of Terms

A

abandonment clause a provision in marine insurance policies allowing an insured company to claim a loss even when property has been abandoned. This clause provides that property must be so substantially damaged that the cost of recovery will exceed its value; or that rehabilitation would cost more than the restored value (a constructive total loss). See also *constructive total loss; marine insurance; surrender value.*

absolute assignment the granting of rights in a policy, to another party or company. For example, a policyowner assigns a lender as partial beneficiary as security for a loan. See also *assignment; collateral assignment; life insurance; ownership rights; policyowner.*

absolute liability the existence of liability even when fault is not established. No-fault liability is practiced in several states. For example, the manufacturer of a product is sued due to injuries caused by that product. Under the absolute liability rule, the manufacturer may be held liable even though no negligence is proven. See also *liability; no-fault.*

absolute ownership the right held by a policyowner to give away or sell the rights in a policy. These include selection of beneficiaries, assignment of rights, and other provisions. See also *absolute assignment; assignment; collateral assignment; ownership rights; policyowner.*

accelerated option the option allowed to a policyowner to apply current cash value and dividends to mature a policy before the scheduled maturity date. See also *cash value; dividend; maturity value.*

accelerated paid-up endowment the application of accumulated dividends to advance a maturity date on a policy. See also *dividend accumulation; endowment; paid-up insurance.*

1

acceptance agreement to an offer made. In an insurance contract, the insurance company accepts an offer made by an applicant who submits an initial premium with an application; or the applicant accepts an offer made by an insurance company quoting the rates and other terms under which it offers a policy. See also *contract; offer.*

accident and health broadly descriptive of lines of insurance including protection against losses arising from accidental death, injury or disability; and from sickness. See also *group health; health insurance.*

accident frequency reference to the occurrence of accidents in a particular location or situation, also known as the experience of a company. The calculation is used to estimate claims levels and, thus, to set premiums. See also *experience.*

accident severity an experience estimate, in which the total claims cost of accidents is predicted in order to establish premium levels. See also *actuarial gain/loss; experience.*

accident year statistics the means of predicting trends in loss experience of a company. The actual losses in a one-year period are expressed as percentages of total premiums paid, to isolate the basic premium required to cover costs. If the statistical trend is on the rise, future premiums must be greater to cover future losses. See also *experience.*

accidental death a death from other than natural causes, for which insurance coverage is often provided at a higher rate than the stated amount in the policy. This provision is also called double indemnity. See also *death benefit; double indemnity.*

accidental death and dismemberment benefits to be paid under the terms of a policy for loss of life or dismemberment due to accidental causes. The policy specifies a benefit for each type of loss from other than natural causes. See also *benefit; death benefit; dismemberment benefit.*

accommodation line insurance underwritten by a company as a courtesy to an agent or agency, when that company would not otherwise accept those risks. The purpose is to capture other, more profitable business also written by the same agent. See also *agent; substandard risk; underwriting.*

accumulated cost a comparison between the cost of insurance and the cost to beneficiaries of providing an equal benefit in the event of loss.

The purpose is to demonstrate the value of carrying life insurance. See also *death benefit; life insurance.*

accumulated dividends   the dividends payable in a participating policy, that are left on deposit to accumulate at compound interest. See also *compound interest; dividend; participating policy.*

accumulated value   a deposited or invested sum of money of the collective periodic payments, plus all interest earned. See also *cash value; compound interest.*

accumulation benefits   **(1)** additional benefits given to the insured in a life insurance policy as part of the original agreement, or as exercise of a participating dividend option. **(2)** the amount of expenses that must be paid during an accumulation period equal to a deductible amount in a health insurance policy, before claims will be paid by the company. See also *deductible; health insurance; life insurance.*

acquisition cost   the total cost to an insurance company of obtaining new business. This includes all marketing expenses, agents' commissions, underwriting, and administrative expenses. See also *commission; load; underwriting gain/loss.*

act of God   a natural loss, one caused not by the actions of individuals or man-made equipment, but from weather and other natural causes. See also *casualty insurance; natural loss.*

active life reserves   reserves on the books of insurance companies to predict the present value of future death claims. On average, the level reserve per policy will be overstated during the early years, when claims are low, and understated later on, when claims will tend to rise. See also *claim; death benefit; life insurance; reserve.* See illustration, page 4.

Actual Cash Value (ACV)   a form of property and casualty insurance that reimburses losses on the basis of current value, less depreciation. For example, a stereo system originally costing $1,200 is lost in a fire. The insurance company determines that, due to wear and tear, the actual cash value has declined to $500. With replacement cost insurance, the actual current replacement cost would be paid, regardless of depreciated value. However, that alternative form of insurance is written with limitations tied to actual cash value. See also *casualty insurance; depreciation; property and casualty insurance; replacement cost.* See illustration, page 4.

active life reserves

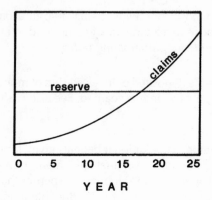

Actual Cash Value (ACV)

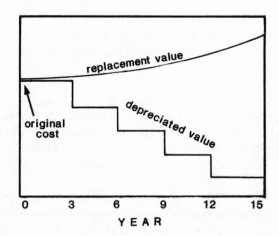

actuarial adjustments revisions in the level of reserves or in required premiums, based upon the company's experience and estimated future claims. See also *expected mortality; experience; loss reserves; reserve.*

actuarial equivalent the comparison of two unlike factors on a mathematical basis. For example, two different policies may be offered for the same premium, but with varying benefits based on the age of the insured and the number of years the company will be at risk. Present and future values are also forms of equivalents. The present value of a future benefit to be paid under a policy will vary with the period of time, the amount at risk, assumptions about the timing of claims, and the assumed interest rate. See also *accumulated value; present value; probability.*

actuarial gain/loss the experience of an insurance company in past and estimated future claims. When actual claims are lower than those estimated, the result is an actuarial gain. See also *experience.*

actuarial present value an estimate of the current value of future benefits, allowing for the probability of claims and chances of a policy remaining in force for the entire period. See also *present value.*

actuary insurance professional responsible for the calculation of probabilities. This individual must estimate reserves based on average policy experience, set premiums for each type of policy, establish dividend rates to be paid on participating policies, and participate in the development of new products by the company. Actuaries may provide statistical information for rate setting on insurance, annuity and retirement products. See also *Fellow, Society of Actuaries (FSA); law of large numbers; probability.*

additional death benefit benefit provided in the event that death occurs during a specific period of years, or from the result of specified causes. See also *benefit; death benefit; double indemnity.*

additional deposit provision a clause in certain whole life insurance policies allowing the insured to make unscheduled premium payments. This provision is common in policies paying variable rates of interest on deposited premiums, or allowing for the purchase of additional insurance coverage. See also *current assumptions; whole life insurance.*

additional insured an individual protected under the terms of a policy, who is not the primary insured. For example, a life insurance policy covers both the insured and a spouse under some conditions. Or, an automobile policy includes protection for a driver other than the primary policyholder.

See also *insured; life insurance; policyholder; property and casualty insurance.*

additional living expenses a benefit included in a homeowner's insurance policy, that will pay for temporary lodging in the event a residence cannot be occupied after a casualty. See also *casualty insurance; homeowner's insurance.*

adhesion contract a form of contract in which the standard provisions offered are not subject to negotiation. In an insurance contract, for example, the policyholder must adhere to the terms and conditions as set forth, and cannot bargain for better benefits, lower rates or other adjustments. See also *contract; standard form.*

adjustable life a hybrid form of life insurance, in which the insured can modify the amount of insurance, rates, and time of coverage. An adjustable life policy contains elements of term and whole life insurance. See also *term life; whole life insurance.*

adjustable premium a form of policy in which the insurer is allowed to modify the premium based upon its claim experience, scope of coverage, and other factors. For example, a group health insurer agrees to cover a group. However, based upon its claims history with that and similarly sized groups, the company may increase or decrease its premium rate at periodic intervals. See also *contract; experience modification.*

adjuster an individual who establishes property and casualty settlement offers in behalf of the insurer. The adjuster may serve as an employee or as an independent service provider. See also *claim; property and casualty insurance; settlement.*

adjustment income a major reason for the purchase of life insurance. Upon the premature or unexpected death of the insured, the beneficiary receives a benefit. When used to support a family until the surviving spouse is able to obtain employment, it is known as adjustment income. See also *beneficiary; death benefit; life insurance.*

Administrative Services Only (ASO) descriptive of the services provided by an insurer or an independent agency. The firm will administer claims and benefit payments for another insurer or a self-employed group, for a fee. See also *benefit; claim; self-insurance.*

administrator   an individual responsible for the probate of an estate, when the insured was intestate. See also *executor; fiduciary; intestate.*

admitted assets   assets of an insurance company that are included in the adjusted balance sheet for statutory purposes. Not all assets are admitted under statutory accounting rules. As a general rule, cash, real estate, securities and other tangible assets are admitted. Non-admitted assets include agents' debit balances and intangible assets. See also *annual statement; non-admitted assets; statutory accounting.*

admitted company   an insurance company licensed to conduct business in a particular state. See also *insurer; statutory requirements.*

advance funding   the funding of a pension plan or other retirement plan in advance of retirement dates. Advance funding is made on the basis of the present value of estimated future retirement benefits the fund is required to pay. See also *pension plan; present value; retirement plan.*

advance premium   the dollar amount of premiums paid in advance of due date. Premiums are earned only during the applicable period. For example, a policyholder pays on the annual mode, so that an entire year's premium is submitted to the company. During the first month of the one-year period, 11/12ths of the total received is advance premium, and only 1/12th is earned. See also *annual premium; earned premium; modal premium; premium.*

---

advance premium

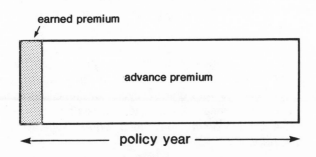

adverse selection   the inclination of an individual to seek insurance or to keep insurance in force when that person knows the risk is high to the company. For example, an individual in poor health is more likely to keep a policy in force, than one whose health is good. Underwriters are aware of adverse selection in the evaluation of risks at the time applications are received. In establishing reserve levels and premiums required to cover future claims, adverse selection must be considered by the insurance company. See also *health insurance; life insurance; renewal premium; risk selection; uninsurable risk.*

affiliated company   insurance companies that are owned by a single holding company or common stockholders, even though they may operate independently. See also *insurer; stock company.*

age limit   the highest and lowest ages at which an insurance company will accept applications. For example, a health or life insurance company policy may stipulate that it will not insure individuals under age one or above age 60. See also *renewal clause; underwriting.*

age setback   the difference in mortality between men and women. Traditionally, insurers have recognized that women outlive men by approximately three years. Thus, the rates charged for women are set at three years before their current age. For example, a woman aged 34 will be charged the same rate as a man aged 31. See also *rate; standard risk.*

agency   concept in law governing the practices of agents and principals. A principal appoints one or more agents to sell insurance and provide services to customers. The principal is responsible for the statements and acts of agents performing within the scope of authorization specified in the agency agreement. See also *captive agent; General Agent (GA); independent agent.*

agency agreement   the contract between a principal and an agent, specifying the terms of the relationship and compensation to be paid. See also *commission; contract.*

agent   an individual insurance salesperson, operating in behalf of an agency or directly for an insurance company. An independent agent may place customers' business with one of several insurance companies with whom it has a contract, while a direct writer represents only one company. See also *captive agent; commission; direct writer; General Agent (GA); licensed agent; principal.*

agent of record   the individual who originally contacted a customer and sold an insurance policy. In the event that individual leaves the agency or company and the business is assigned to a replacement, the agency agreement might specify that the agent of record will continue to receive part of the renewal commissions on that policy. See also *application; commission; contract.*

aggregate indemnity   the maximum dollar amount an individual is allowed to collect in benefits, under the terms of an insurance contract, or on all policies the individual owns. For example, health and disability policies set maximum benefit payments that will be allowed under contract terms. See also *coverage; disability benefit; indemnity; risk.*

aggregate limit   the maximum benefit to be paid on a property and casualty policy, or under a health insurance policy, either per occurrence or for the entire policy. Upon reaching that limit, the policy terminates. See also *health insurance; liability insurance; noncancellable guaranteed renewable; risk.*

aleatory contract   a form of contract in which both sides understand that values will not necessarily be equal. In an insurance contract, for example, the insured might pay premiums for many years without receiving benefits; or the insurer might be required to pay out a large claim without collecting more than the first premium. An aleatory contract is one entered into with the knowledge that unknown future events will affect relative benefits to each side. See also *benefit; contract; premium.*

all risks   the most extensive form of homeowner's insurance, covering all risks except named exclusions, also known as HO-3. See also *casualty insurance; HO-3; homeowner's insurance; named perils.*

allied lines   extended forms of property and casualty insurance, often provided in addition to basic fire insurance in commercial policies. Coverage may include protection against loss to data processing equipment and records, earthquakes, vandalism, water and leakage insurance, and a wide number of other possible casualties. See also *casualty insurance; fire insurance; property and casualty insurance.*

allocated benefits   form of benefits specified by itemization in the contract itself, to specified maximums or payable under certain conditions. See also *benefit; risk.*

allowable charge   a term used in Medicare, representing a reasonable limit on services. The covered amount is 80% of the usual and customary fee. See also *health insurance; Medicare; Usual, Customary and Reasonable (UCR).*

amendment   a change in terms of a policy, either to extend coverage or to add an additional form of insurance. For example, a homeowner's policy is modified to include insurance on business equipment in a home office. See also *contract; endorsement; policy; rider.*

American Academy of Actuaries (AAA)   an organization of professional insurance actuaries. Members are entitled to certify documents filed with the Internal Revenue Service, the Department of Labor, and other government agencies. See also *actuary.*

American College (AC)   the organization that tests underwriting professionals, and awards the designations Chartered Financial Consultant (ChFC) and Chartered Life Underwriter (CLU). The College was previously called the American College of Life Underwriters. See also *Chartered Financial Consultant (ChFC); Chartered Life Underwriter (CLU); underwriting.*

American Council of Life Insurance (ACLI)   a lobbying organization consisting of member insurance companies. The Council distributes information to the general public, researches the life insurance industry, and consults with regulatory agencies. See also *life insurance.*

American Institute for Property and Liability Underwriters (AIPLU)   an organization that accredits members for the Chartered Property and Casualty Underwriter (CPCU) designation, and offers correspondence courses and continuing education in the underwriting field. See also *Chartered Property and Casualty Underwriter (CPCU); liability insurance; property and casualty insurance; underwriting.*

American Insurance Association (AIA)   an organization consisting of property and casualty insurance company members, that promotes accounting, regulatory and industry practice standards. See also *property and casualty insurance.*

American Risk and Insurance Association (ARIA)   an association of companies and individuals in the insurance profession, providing research and education in the area of risk management. ARIA also publishes the Journal of Risk and Insurance. See also *risk management.*

American Society of Chartered Life Underwriters (ASCLU)   an association whose members hold the Chartered Life Underwriter (CLU) license, that offers continuing education services and information for the general public. See also *Chartered Life Underwriter (CLU); underwriting.*

amount at risk   **(1)** for life insurance policies, the difference between the face value and the amount set up as a reserve against future claims for the same policy. **(2)** in property and casualty insurance, the maximum possible claim or the stated policy limit. See also *face amount; life insurance; property and casualty insurance; reserve value; risk.*

amount at risk

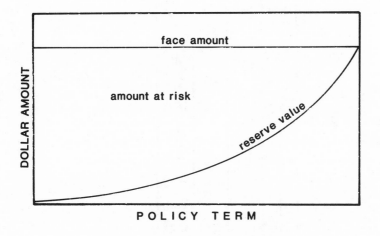

ancillary benefits   benefits provided in a health insurance policy for expenses such as drugs, surgical dressings, ambulance service, tests and anesthetic. See also *benefit; health insurance; hospitalization insurance.*

anniversary date   the yearly date corresponding to the effective date of issue of a policy. This date is significant in the establishment of reserves, statistical analysis of retention and lapse studies, and calculation of annual reserves. See also *date of issue; policy anniversary.*

annual premium a premium paid on an annual basis, as opposed to semi-annual, quarterly or monthly modes; or a modal premium expressed in annual terms (four times a quarterly premium, for example). See also *modal premium; premium.*

---

annual premium

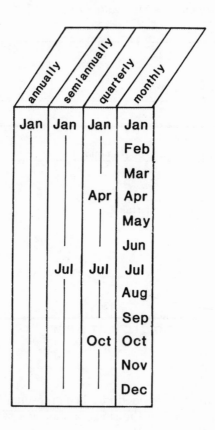

---

annual statement also called the convention blank, a detailed financial summary that is filed by every insurance company. The annual statement is sent to the domicile state's insurance commissioner, and a copy is submitted to every state in which the company is licensed to operate. Included in the report are assets, liabilities and net worth; a statement of operations; business reported by lines; reserves; investments; record of earnings of highly compensated employees; claims and pending claims; information on participating dividends; and a breakdown of business by state. See also *convention blank; National Association of Insurance Commissioners (NAIC).*

annuitant an individual who owns an annuity policy written by an insurance company, and is entitled to benefits under the terms of that contract. See also *benefit; policyowner.*

annuity a contract written by an insurance company, to provide income benefits for a specified number of years, or for life. While a life insurance contract insures against the economic consequences of death, an annuity provides income guarantees while the annuitant is alive. A sum of money is paid, either over a period of years (known as the accumulation period) or in a single premium. Upon annuitization, usually at age 65, the individual receives monthly or quarterly payments. Some annuities guarantee a minimum payment with potential for variable rates based on investment return. An annuity may provide for payments over a specified period of time (an annuity certain), or for the remainder of a person's life. See also *accumulation benefits; cash refund annuity; fixed dollar annuity; installment refund annuity; joint life and survivors annuity; life annuity certain; liquidation period; pure annuity; variable dollar annuity.*

---

annuity

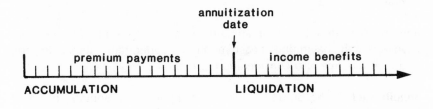

annuity certain a form of annuity in which payments are guaranteed to the annuitant for a specified period of time. In the event the annuitant expires prior to this period, the remainder of the guaranteed payments are made to a named beneficiary. If the annuitant lives beyond the guaranteed period, life annuity certain payments continue indefinitely. See also *beneficiary; certain payment; life annuity certain.*

---

annuity certain

annuity consideration the premium payments under an annuity contract, made as installments over a period of years, or in a lump sum. See also *consideration; premium.*

annuity due descriptive of an annuity contract calling for premium payments at the beginning of each month or quarter, rather than at the end of the period. See also *consideration; premium.*

annuity factor the present value in a temporary life annuity, of future benefit payments. The insurer calculates its likely future liability, given the annuitant's present age, life expectancy, terms of the contract, and assumed rate of interest it will earn. See also *present value; temporary life annuity.* See illustration, page 15.

annuity table a mortality table used to set the rates for annuity contracts. Based upon the averages for the annuitant's age and sex, the insurer

annuity factor

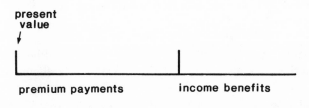

estimates the number alive at the beginning of each year, and the number estimated to die during that year. The average life expectancy then indicates the appropriate premium for a given age. See also *life expectancy; mortality table; probability.*

apparent authority   the authority an agent is presumed to have under the terms of an agency agreement. See also *agency agreement.*

application   a written statement completed by an applicant for insurance, providing financial and health history for the underwriting process. The company may investigate the statements made on the application before issuing a policy. The application is considered as part of the insurance contract. Any fraudulent statements, if discovered, will nullify the contract at any time during its term. See also *risk selection; underwriting.*

appraisal   the valuation of damages or property for the purpose of setting insurance levels or settling a claim. See also *casualty insurance; claim.*

approval   the process of accepting an offer (if the insured submitted an initial premium), or of making an offer for an insurance contract, on the basis of information supplied on an application. See also *policy; risk selection; underwriting.*

arbitration   the settlement of differences between an insurer and the insured, by submitting to the findings of a neutral third party (or parties). An arbitration clause in an insurance policy specifies that disagreements will be settled through binding arbitration, as an alternative to litigation. See also *claim; settlement.*

assessable mutual company a form of mutual insurance company (in which policyowners own the company) allowed to assess additional premiums when losses exceed previous estimates. Depending upon the state involved, assessments for each type of risk may be limited by law. See also *mutual company; risk.*

assessed value the estimated current value of property, either for insurance or tax purposes. See also *depreciation; replacement; settlement.*

assessment company an insurer that is allowed to assess additional charges to policyowners, rather than being restricted to a fixed premium for a specific type of insurance coverage. The assessment will vary with the actual loss experience. See also *fixed premium; insurer.*

Asset Share Value (ASV) **(1)** the proportional value a participating policyowner has of the company's net assets, calculated for each class of insurance. The gross premiums are reduced by expenses and dividends paid. **(2)** the calculation of required reserves for a line of insurance, based upon known past claims and future estimated claims and assumed interest rates. See also *experience; life insurance; reserve value.*

assigned risk automobile insurance coverage provided as a matter of law, to individuals who would not otherwise qualify for standard coverage. Each insurer in a state participates in the pool, charging a rated premium as part of the assigned risk pool. See also *automobile insurance; pool; rated policy.*

assignment the transfer of rights under a life insurance policy to another individual or a company. For example, in order to secure a loan, a borrower will assign cash values or partial beneficiary rights to the lender, until the loan has been repaid. See also *absolute assignment; cash value; collateral assignment; life insurance.*

assignment clause a provision in a life insurance policy naming another person as beneficiary or recipient of other benefits. See also *beneficiary; contract; life insurance; policyowner.*

Association for Advanced Life Underwriting (AALU) an organization associated with the National Association of Life Underwriters (NALU), with membership limited to individual professionals with many years of underwriting experience. See also *National Association of Life Underwriters (NALU); underwriting.*

association group   holders of a group insurance policy belonging to one or more associations or trade groups. In order for a group to form, the members must have a collective feature or interests. See also *group health; health insurance; master policy.*

attained age   the age of an insured individual, used as a point of identification. For example, a policy is issued at the age of 35. The policy stipulates that the policy can be renewed at the attained age of 45. See also *conversion; life expectancy; original age.*

attorney in fact   an individual who represents the interests of another, also said to have power of attorney. See also *agency; power of attorney.*

authorized company   an insurance company that is licensed to conduct business in a particular state. See also *insurer; unauthorized insurer.*

automatic premium loan   a provision in a whole life insurance policy, stating that due premiums will be paid by way of an automatic loan upon expiration of a grace period. In the event the policyowner does not make payments by that date, the company will grant the loan, offsetting cash value to make the payment. The provision will be exercised only if cash value is adequate to make the payment. Otherwise, the policy will lapse. See also *cash value; grace period; life insurance; premium loan; surrender value; whole life insurance.*

automatic reinstatement   a clause in a property and casualty insurance policy, stating that the full face value of the policy will be restored after a claim has been paid, under specified conditions. See also *property and casualty insurance; reinstatement.*

automobile insurance   coverage on personal or business use of a motor vehicle, including protection against loss to property or bodily injury. Also included in the policy is protection against losses due to vandalism or theft from the vehicle. See also *Business Automobile Policy (BAP); Personal Automobile Policy (PAP).*

Average Net Cost (ANC)   the average cost of life insurance over a 20-year period, allowing for dividends (if a participating policy) and cash value at the end of the period. While the method does not provide an actuarial basis for comparison of values, it does enable a policyholder to assess relative values of different insurance policies. Example: premiums over a 20-year period total $8,250. During the same period, dividends total $415 and cash value will be $6,604. The annual ANC is $61.55 (premiums less dividends and cash value, divided by 20). See also *cash value; dividend; life insurance; non-participating policy; participating policy.*

Average Net Cost (ANC)

20 years:

total premiums	$8,250
less:	
dividends	$ 415
cash value	6,604
	$7,019
net cost	$1,231
ANC	$ 61.55

---

avoidance   a concept in risk management, that the insured will reduce exposure to loss by avoiding exposure. For example, a company especially vulnerable to product liability lawsuits may cease manufacturing a particular product. See also *risk management.*

B

back-end load   a form of insurance or annuity contract in which expenses are deducted not at the time of sale, but in future years or upon withdrawal from the contract. The spreading of expenses over a period of years is a disincentive to removing money from the contract, and is also used as a sales argument. Load is the charging of expenses, including a salesperson's commission. In comparing a front-end and back-end load contract, they may be equally loaded. However, the back-load will appear to be a better buy because expenses are not deducted at the time the contract is entered. See also *front-end load; gross premium; load; net premium.*

basic policy   a form of homeowner's insurance in which only minimal casualty protection is offered. Only 11 named perils are included, to the exclusion of all other losses. The policy is also called HO-1. See also *casualty insurance; HO-1; homeowner's insurance; liability insurance; named perils.*

beneficiary   in a life insurance policy, trust or will, the individual who will receive benefits upon the death of the insured. The policyowner in a life insurance contract designates the primary beneficiary as well as any secondary or contingent beneficiaries. See also *contingent beneficiary; life insurance; primary beneficiary; trust; will.*

beneficiary clause   a section of the life insurance contract in which the beneficiary is named. The policyowner may change the beneficiary by writing to the insurer. However, an irrevocable beneficiary (in an insurance contract or trust) cannot be changed without the permission of the person originally named). See also *contract; irrevocable beneficiary; life insurance; revocable beneficiary.*

beneficiary of trust   the person or persons named as recipients of a trust, for whom the trust was set up. See also *irrevocable beneficiary; revocable beneficiary; trust.*

benefit   the amount of money an insured or a beneficiary receives upon submission of a legitimate claim. A benefit may also take the form of rights, such as the right to renew a policy under favorable conditions; to add additional coverage; or to select settlement options. See also *claim; coverage; indemnity.*

benefit formula   the method of calculating benefits in a retirement plan or under a group insurance plan. The calculation determines the benefit accrued to each participant. See also *employee; pension plan; retirement plan.*

benefit period   under the terms of a health insurance program or Medicare, the term from which benefits begin to accrue; or the total period of time that benefits will be paid, after which the insurance coverage ceases. See also *health insurance; Medicare.*

bilateral contract   a contract that involves equal consideration by both sides. For example, an insurance contract is an exchange of protection (and, ultimately, benefits) in return for premiums paid by the policyowner. See also *acceptance; consideration; contract; insurance contract; offer; unilateral contract.*

binder an agreement to provide insurance, pending the issue of a more complete and formal contract. Property and casualty insurance is often sold by way of a verbal binder. See also *contract; property and casualty insurance.*

binding receipt a receipt given to the insured upon submission of the initial premium. This is a conditional contract. If the insured is approved as a risk by the underwriting department, the insurance policy is enforceable from the time the receipt is given. See also *conditional receipt; initial premium.*

blanket contract any form of insurance involving multiple coverages. It may take several forms. The property of one company or person can be insured at several different locations. Or several individuals may be covered under a single group life or health policy. See also *contract; health insurance; life insurance; property and casualty insurance.*

blanket medical clause a provision in a health insurance policy specifying that the benefits under the contract are payable to a stated maximum; but that no limits are placed on specific classes of expense. See also *health insurance.*

bodily injury liability coverage a class of automobile insurance that protects the policyholder against the cost of injuries to another person. See also *automobile insurance; liability insurance.*

bond a form of insurance against financial losses arising from the conduct of business. For example, a fidelity bond provides suretyship against losses from thefts by employees. See also *fidelity bond; surety bond.*

borderline risk a risk that is minimally acceptable to the insurance company, but that might be underwritten as an accommodation to an agency that is also bringing in other, more desirable business. See also *accommodation line; risk selection.*

broad form a type of homeowner's insurance, also known as HO-2, providing casualty protection for 18 named perils. See also *casualty insurance; HO-2; homeowner's insurance; liability insurance; named perils.*

broker   used interchangeably with "agent," but more often descriptive of an independent agent. See also *agent; General Agent (GA); licensed agent.*

broker-agent   an individual who sells insurance and also offers to seek the best possible forms of coverage for customers, also called an independent agent or an insurance broker. See also *agent; independent agent.*

Business Automobile Policy (BAP)   a policy covering a range of losses in connection with the business use of a motor vehicle. The policy defines the range of coverages included, such as geographic limits, types of casualties and liabilities, and dollar amounts and ceilings on protection. The policy includes liability insurance for damages incurred while operating the vehicle, with stated exceptions. It also includes physical damage insurance of two types: comprehensive insurance (damage from fire, theft, and other identified events) and collision (damage resulting directly from collisions with other vehicles or objects, or from turning over). See also *automobile insurance; collision coverage; comprehensive insurance; liability insurance.*

business liability   protection against damages resulting from the conduct of business. Protection takes two forms: direct liability (resulting from the actions of employees or conditions of products or property) and contingent liability (potential damages in the future). See also *contingent liability; direct liability; liability insurance.*

Business Owner's Policy (BOP)   a form of insurance designed for the small business owner. It provides protection against damages to business property and those arising from bodily injuries to other people. In order to qualify, the work space and number of floors in a building are restricted; and certain types of businesses (such as bars, restaurants, banks, contractors, and manufacturers) do not qualify. See also *liability insurance; property and casualty insurance.*

business risk exclusion   a clause in a liability policy specifying that the insurance excludes protection when products are misrepresented. For example, a manufacturer claims that a product is safe under specified conditions, and suit is brought because the claim is false. The business risk exclusion will not reimburse damages arising in those conditions. See also *exclusion; liability insurance.*

buy-sell agreement   an agreement between partners in a partnership, major stockholders in a corporation, or the owner and a key employee in a sole proprietorship. The buy-sell (or buy out) agreement specifies that, in the event of the death or disability of one or more owners, the remaining owners (or key employees) will purchase their interests in the business. This prevents ownership from passing out of the hands of the principals. The agreement involves the setting of a formula for value of the business at the time of death or disability, and may also call for the purchase of life or disability insurance. The proceeds of the insurance policy are to be used to purchase interests of the insured individual. See also *disability buy-out; key employee insurance; life insurance.*

C

cafeteria plan   a form of employee benefit plan in which each employee is allowed to divide a total dollar amount between several available benefits. For example, a married employee's spouse may already provide adequate health and life insurance from another employer. Under a cafeteria plan, the employee might assign a majority of the available dollars to a retirement plan, disability income insurance, and other benefits. See also *benefit; employee; group contract.* See illustration, page 23.

cancellation provision   the right or limit of rights to cancel a contract. An insurer may not cancel a policy as long as premiums are paid, if that policy includes a noncancellable feature. It must renew the policy but may increase premiums under a guaranteed renewable contract. Life insurance policy provisions cannot be changed and the coverage cannot be stopped as long as premium payments continue, for the specified term of insurance. The insured can cancel a policy of insurance at any time by stopping payment of premiums. See also *expiration; guaranteed renewable; lapse; noncancellable guaranteed renewable.*

capacity   **(1)** the mental ability to comprehend an action, which must be present in order for a contract to be considered valid. **(2)** the ceiling an insurance company places on its risks for each policy, also called the retention limit. For example, an insurer places a $25,000 capacity on any one policy. An individual purchases $50,000 of life insurance, and the excess is ceded to a reinsurance company. Under the terms of the agreement, the risk is limited and shared. Premiums received by the original insurer will be shared with the reinsurer on an agreed-upon basis. See also *contract; reinsurance; retention; risk selection.* See illustration, page 23.

capital   the net worth of a corporation, partnership or individual, or the difference between total assets and total liabilities. An insurance company's

cafeteria plan

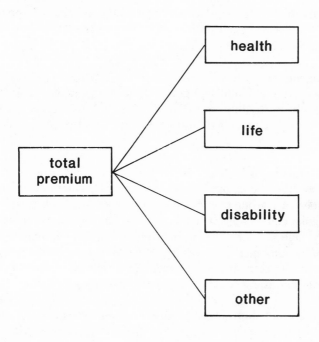

capacity

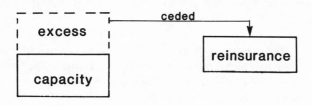

capital excludes non-admitted assets. See also *admitted assets; net worth; non-admitted assets; stock company.*

capital needs analysis descriptive of a process used to sell insurance, notably by agents who consider themselves to be financial planners. The technique involves a series of assumptions about financial needs in the future, including an allowance for an estimated rate of inflation. This future need, combined with the risks associated with loss of earning power (from death, disability or health problems) is the premise for selling insurance coverage. See also *financial plan.*

captive agent   an agent who, by contract, is allowed to sell insurance for only one company or affiliated group. This arrangement is more prevalent in life, health and disability lines than in casualty insurance, where independent agency agreements are more common. See also *agent; independent agent.*

captive company   a company that provides coverage in one industry or for one group only. The company may be formed by parent organizations or, collectively, by a group of companies in one industry. This practice occurs when regular commercial insurance is either unavailable or the cost is prohibitively high. In some forms of captive company formation, the risk spreading is combined with self-insurance in varying degrees. Premiums paid to a captive company are tax deductible, whereas reserves established to provide self-insurance are not. See also *self-insurance.*

care, custody and control   a provision in a liability insurance policy specifying an exclusion from coverage. See also *liability insurance.*

cash refund annuity   a form of annuity policy in which a lump sum distribution is made if the annuitant dies before completion of the cash refund period. The annuity guarantees a minimum number of payments. However, when the annuitant dies, the lump sum refund is made to the named beneficiary. See also *annuity; lump sum distribution; settlement option.*

cash value   the savings portion of a whole life insurance policy. Such policies contain two elements: insurance and cash value. The two elements always equal the policy's face amount; as the cash value increases over time, the insurance portion declines by the same amount. By maturity of the policy, the entire face amount is represented by cash value. If the policy is surrendered before maturity, the insured is entitled to a sum of cash, known as the cash surrender value. The insured person is also entitled to a policy loan to the amount of cash value available. See also *life insurance; surrender value; whole life insurance.*

Casualty Actuarial Society (CAS)   a professional association that awards members the designation of Fellow, Casualty Actuarial Society (FCAS). This is granted following a series of examinations on the math and financial aspects of casualty insurance. See also *actuary; Fellow, Casualty Actuarial Society (FCAS).*

casualty insurance   protection against the economic losses that may result from unexpected and unpredictable occurrences, known also as acts of God; and, in a broader application, all lines of insurance protecting the insured individual or company from the monetary assessments of damages resulting from negligence and other forms of liability to others. See also *act of God; liability; personal injury.*

catastrophic loss   an unpredictable occurrence that will cause significant financial loss or hardship to an individual or company. To protect against such an event, one might put away a sum of money as a reserve, as a form of self-insurance. In cases where the cost of insurance is prohibitively high, a group of firms in one industry may form a self-insurance pool. But in many cases, self-insurance is too risky to serve as a viable alternative. In these cases, insurance is a form of protection against uncertainty, in the realization that, should a loss occur, the cost would exceed the cost of mitigating the risk. For example, a homeowner could lose most of the equity in a home if a fire occurred; or a business could lose millions of dollars in equipment, inventory and information due to a fire, other natural disaster, or theft. The purpose of insurance is to spread the risk of catastrophic loss among a large number of insured parties. It is a statistical certainty that such losses will occur in a certain percentage of cases. The insurer collects premiums from all the insured to cover the claims of the few. And for the insured, the premium is the price of protection against the possibility of a loss. See also *risk management; self-insurance.*

ceding company   an insurer that transfers part of its risk to another, called a reinsurance company. Each insurer sets retention limits, a ceiling on the degree of risk it is willing to underwrite on a single case. When policies exceed that limit, the excess is ceded. A portion of the risk is transferred, along with a portion of the premiums received on that policy. See also *reinsurance ceded; retention; risk.*

certain payment   a payment that will be made in the future, without exception. For example, the cash value on a whole life policy will be paid out as a matured benefit, as a surrender value, or in the form of a policy loan. And the liquidation benefits in an annuity contract may include a guaranteed minimum number of payments. Even if the annuitant deceases prior to expiration of that term, the balance is a certain payment, and will be paid to the beneficiary. See also *annuity certain; cash value.*

certificate of authority a statement allowing an insurance company to offer certain, specified lines of insurance within a state, granted by the Commissioner of Insurance of that state; or a written authorization given by the company to an agent or agents, specifying the rights granted in representing the company in selling insurance and servicing customers in a specified area. See also *agent; Commissioner of Insurance; licensed agent.*

certificate of convenience a temporary license granted to an agent-to-be, allowing that individual to sell insurance until a proper, permanent license is obtained. The certificate may be given to someone currently studying for the state insurance exam, or to a newly employed agent in training. See also *agent; licensed agent; temporary license.*

certificate of insurance a document evidencing insurance in a group plan. It assigns an individual and a group number, summarizes major benefits and limitations, and identifies the insured member of the group. A more detailed listing of policy provisions is included in a master policy. See also *coverage; group health; master policy.*

Certified Employee Benefit Specialist (CEBS) a professional designation awarded to qualified individuals specializing in employee benefit sales and administration. This designation is granted by the International Foundation of Employee Benefit Plans. Tests are given in Social Security, health insurance, retirement planning, group plans, labor relations, and other employment-related subjects. Testing is administered by the Wharton School. See also *benefit; employee.*

Certified Financial Planner (CFP) a license granted by the College for Financial Planning, upon completion of a series of examinations. A financial planner should work with individuals to design a plan suited specifically to individual needs; in practice, a large number of individuals use the title to sell insurance products or mutual funds. The certification program is an attempt to establish professional credentials in an otherwise unregulated field. See also *financial planner.*

change of beneficiary the right of a policyowner to replace one named beneficiary with another in a life insurance policy. The assignment of an individual is generally revocable by the policyowner, unless designated as an irrevocable provision. See also *beneficiary; irrevocable beneficiary; life insurance; revocable beneficiary.*

change of plan a benefit in some insurance policies allowing the policyholder to convert to another plan, often without additional requirements.

The new plan may involve a change in premiums. For example, the holder of a term life insurance policy has the right to renew on a more favorable basis, to increase the amount of insurance, or to convert to a cash value form of coverage, without being required to undergo a medical exam. See also *adverse selection; convertible term; policy.*

Chartered Financial Analyst (CFA)   a designation awarded by the Institute of Chartered Financial Analysts, to members with five or more years' experience in finance, economics, accounting, and financial planning. To win the designation, the member passes a series of three exams. See also *financial planner.*

Chartered Financial Consultant (ChFC)   a designation awarded by the American College (AC), requiring successful passage of a series of exams in insurance, finance, taxation, employee benefits, management, accounting and investments. See also *American College (AC); financial planner.*

Chartered Life Underwriter (CLU)   a nationally recognized professional designation for underwriters, awarded by the American College (AC) upon completion of a series of examinations. See *American College (AC); underwriting.*

Chartered Property and Casualty Underwriter (CPCU)   a professional designation awarded by the American Institute for Property and Liability Underwriters (AIPLU), after passage of a series of 10 exams; three years of professional experience are also required before the designation is given. See also *American Institute for Property and Liability Underwriters (AIPLU); property and casualty insurance; risk management; underwriting.*

civil damages   monetary awards claimed in a suit or granted as remedy to a successful plaintiff. Civil damages may be general, special or punitive. See also *liability.*

civil liability   a concept of liability for wrongs other than criminal wrongs, including liability arising from negligence and acts or omissions that cause personal injury. See also *negligence; personal injury.*

claim   a demand, request or notice submitted to an insurance company by an insured person or company. The claim asks for benefits under the terms of a policy when a loss has been suffered. The insurance contract specifies that covered losses are either paid or reimbursed by the company. See also *contract; indemnity; insurance contract; loss.*

claims made insurance   a form of liability protection. The contract stipulates that all claims submitted during the period of coverage will be paid. However, claims made after a lapse or termination of the policy will not be paid. This is so even if the loss occurred during the coverage period. Depending upon the terms of a specific claims made contract, the company might be liable for losses that occurred prior to the period of coverage, as long as the claim is made during a coverage period. However, many types of policies will not reimburse for losses that actually occurred before the policy initiation. It is possible that an insured with continuous coverage would not be able to obtain reimbursement. For example, a company changes liability policies in June. In September, a liability suit is filed, for an event that took place the previous February. The previous insurer will deny the claim because the policy has lapsed; and the current insurer will also deny the claim because the loss occurred prior to the period of the policy. See also *liability insurance; property and casualty insurance.*

---

claims made insurance

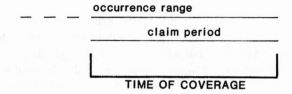

occurrence range

claim period

TIME OF COVERAGE

---

claims occurrence insurance   a form of liability insurance in which losses are payable for any covered event that took place during the period of coverage. This is true even when a loss is not discovered until after lapse or termination of the policy. For example, a company changes insurance carriers in June. In September, a liability suit is filed, for an event that took place the previous February. The previous insurer must pay the claim if the insurance contract was structured on a claims occurrence basis, as the loss took place during the period of coverage. See also *liability insurance; property and casualty insurance.* See illustration, page 29.

claims reserve   a fund set up to pay known claims in the future that have not yet been settled. The delay may occur so that the company can

claims occurrence insurance

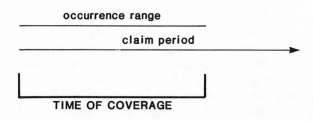

occurrence range

claim period

TIME OF COVERAGE

investigate the amount of the claim, assess actual damages, or gather documentation needed to complete its file. This form of reserve is not an actuarial liability such as a reserve for future claims set up by way of book entry; it is a monetary fund for known, filed claims. It will not include the Incurred But Not Reported (IBNR) liability. That is an estimate of claims that, on average, will be filed in the immediate future, for which the company has not yet been notified. See also *Incurred But Not Reported (IBNR); reserve.*

class a group of insured persons or companies who share common characteristics, such as age, type of insurance, or geographic spread (individuals); or company size or type of coverage (companies). For the purpose of following statistical trends and risk experience, actuaries may track histories or establish reserves by generation, "sets," or classes. See also *experience; insured; rate; risk.*

class rate a premium rate per units of insurance sold in a particular class. For example, a certain type of company located in a state or region might represent a greater risk to the insurer; thus, the premium will be higher for identical coverage in another area or for a different type of company. See also *insured; rate; risk selection.*

classified risk a risk that is other than standard. As a classified, or substandard, risk, the insured will be required to pay a higher premium for the coverage. See also *substandard risk.*

codicil an amendment or attachment to a will. The document changes or adds terms without nullifying the original document. For example, an individual's parent dies and leaves an antique desk to him. His current will leaves all of his possessions to his wife. However, he wants to will the desk to his brother. Without changing his original will, a codicil is prepared naming the brother. See also *will*.

coinsurance **(1)** in health insurance policies, the portion of covered expenses that the insured is required to pay. This applies both to commercial insurance and to Medicare. For example, an individual incurs $4,000 of medical expenses above the deductible. Medicare will pay 80%, or $3,200; the individual is responsible for the coinsurance portion, which is 20%, or $800. This should not be confused with the deductible. After the deductible, the coinsurance relates to all further expenses. **(2)** similar to reinsurance, the sharing of risks between two or more different insurance companies. For example, a company's retention limit is $20,000. A policy is sold for $30,000, and the excess of $10,000 will be ceded to another insurer, often a reinsurance company. In that instance, the two companies coinsure the risk. **(3)** in property and casualty insurance, the total amount of each type of loss the company will pay. The insured is responsible for the excess, or coinsurance above that specified limit. See also *allowable charge; covered expenses; health insurance; Medicare; property and casualty insurance; reinsurance; retention; risk.* See illustrations below and on page 31.

coinsurance (health)

claim amount	$8,415
less: deductible	500
	$7,915
paid, 80%	6,332
coinsurance	$1,583

collateral assignment the appointment of a lender as beneficiary on a life insurance policy. This is limited to the balance outstanding on a loan, and grants the lender a guarantee of full repayment in the event of a borrower's death. The collateral assignment expires upon full repayment of the loan. See also *absolute assignment; assignment; death benefit; life insurance.*

coinsurance (of risk)

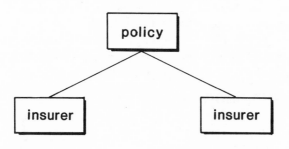

---

collision coverage   insurance against losses incurred when an automobile strikes another object or vehicle, or rolls over. See also *automobile insurance.*

combination agent   an agent who sells two types of insurance. The term is applied specifically to life insurance agents selling both industrial and ordinary life policies. See also *agent; industrial life; ordinary life.*

combination plan   **(1)** a life insurance contract that includes features of both whole life and term insurance. For example, a policy might allow the insured to vary the amount of insurance protection by specified terms. Subsequent additions are charged a premium rate based on the individual's current age. At the same time, the amount of total premium going into cash values can be varied. **(2)** a pension or retirement plan that consists of an investment account and a life insurance contract. See also *adjustable life; life insurance; pension plan; term life; whole life insurance.*

combined ratio   the addition of the loss ratio and the expense ratio, to determine total reductions to gross income. When the combined ratio exceeds 100% in a year, the excess is a loss (without taking into account its return on investments). The loss ratio is a percentage derived by dividing incurred losses by earned premiums. And the expense ratio is a percentage derived by dividing incurred expenses by written premium. For example, one insurer reports the following (in thousands of dollars):

incurred losses	$167,800
earned premium	214,400
incurred expenses	54,800
written premium	355,100

In this example, the loss ratio is 78.3% and the expense ratio is 15.4%. The combined ratio is 93.7%. It is possible for insurers to report a combined ratio in excess of 100% and still report a net profit, if net investment income exceeds the combined ratio's excess above 100 percent. See also *earned premium; expense ratio; Incurred Loss Ratio (ILR); written premium.*

combined ratio

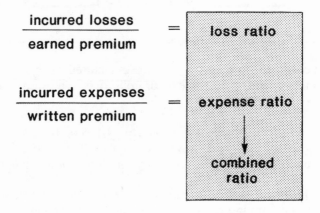

$$\frac{\text{incurred losses}}{\text{earned premium}} = \boxed{\text{loss ratio}}$$

$$\frac{\text{incurred expenses}}{\text{written premium}} = \boxed{\text{expense ratio}}$$

combined ratio

$$\frac{\$167,800}{\$214,400} = \boxed{78.3\%}$$

$$\frac{\$54,800}{\$355,100} = \boxed{15.4\%}$$

93.7%

commercial insurance **(1)** any form of insurance purchased by a business to protect itself against the economic consequences of potential future losses. **(2)** health insurance that includes disability income protection and medical expense provisions. The policy may be renewable at the company's option, or nonrenewable for stated reasons only (such as an age limitation on insured individuals). Some forms are also noncancellable, meaning the contract may not be cancelled or changed in any way as long as the insured continues making premium payments. A policy can also be classified as guaranteed renewable. In that case, the company must continue coverage beyond an identified term, but has the right to increase premiums based on age and claims experience. **(3)** any form of insurance sold by companies operating for a profit, as distinguished from major non-profit insurance providers. See also *business liability; guaranteed renewable; health insurance; noncancellable guaranteed renewable; renewal clause.*

commission the compensation earned by the insurance agent. This commission is expressed as a percentage of the premium paid by the company, and will vary by type of insurance product. The gross premium a policyholder pays includes a load factor for expenses, taxes and agents' commission. However, the load may not cover the first year commission during the first year. When a company will earn a substantial profit over time and wants to emphasize one product over another, it may offer first-year commissions far exceeding 100% of premiums received. Over the term insurance is in force, the company earns a profit by the combination of reduced renewal commissions and profits on its investment activities. See also *agent; first year commission; load.*

Commissioner of Insurance the individual appointed in each state to oversee the activities of insurance companies licensed to operate in that state. The Insurance Department, under the Commissioner, is responsible for evaluating reserve requirements of companies, and for protecting consumers against unfair marketing or claims practices. Activities of the various states are coordinated and standardized by the National Association of Insurance Commissioners (NAIC). Each insurer is required to submit an annual statement (called the convention blank) to the Commissioner in each state in which it operates. See also *convention blank; National Association of Insurance Commissioners (NAIC).*

Commissioners Standard Industrial Mortality Table (CSI) table for calculation of nonforfeiture values on industrial life insurance policies. The rates for insurance are somewhat higher than for ordinary life at the same ages. Historically, purchasers of industrial life have been proven to have shorter life spans. See also *industrial life; life expectancy; life insurance; mortality.*

Commissioners Standard Ordinary Mortality Table (CSO) table for calculation of nonforfeiture values on ordinary life insurance policies. The table reflects the minimum amounts the company must guarantee to its policyholders. See also *life expectancy; life insurance; mortality; ordinary life.*

commissioners value a listing of specific securities and their estimated conservative current values, published each year by the National Association of Securities Commissioners (NAIC). The purpose is to establish uniform valuation among all insurers for the purpose of uniform reporting. Securities not included on the listing may not be reported as admitted assets. See also *annual statement; investment income; Mandatory Securities Valuation Reserve (MSVR); National Association of Insurance Commissioners (NAIC); reserve value.*

common disaster clause a provision in a life insurance contract stating determination of survivorship. This is significant only in cases when the insured and the primary beneficiary die together in a common disaster. In the event that the sequence of death cannot be determined, it is assumed that the insured died last. The order of death determines whether or not a contingent beneficiary is entitled to proceeds under the contract. See also *beneficiary; contingent beneficiary; joint and survivors clause; life insurance; survivorship benefit.*

commutation rights the right held by a beneficiary to take income payments due upon the death of an insured or annuitant, in a lump sum payment. For example, an annuitant is guaranteed a certain number of payments. However, he dies before that period is over. His widow elects to receive the balance due from the insurer in a single payment. See also *beneficiary; lump sum distribution; settlement option.*

commuted value the present value of a specific number of future payments, also called the discounted value. In computing the premium required for a future annuity, for example, the commuted value is derived based on several factors: the period of time between the premium payment and annuitization; the number of payments to be made under the contract; and the assumed rate of interest the insurer will be able to earn on the deposited sum. See also *discount; interest assumption; present value; sinking fund.* See illustration, page 35.

comparative negligence a concept in tort law in which two or more defendants may share negligence in relative degrees. There is a clear distinction between comparative and contributory negligence (a concept that someone

commuted value

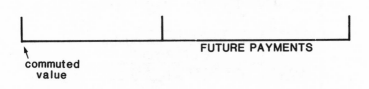

FUTURE PAYMENTS

commuted
value

---

bringing suit may be partially responsible, and shares negligence with the accused party). An example of comparative negligence: suit is brought against two defendants, a manufacturer and a distributor. Total liability is assigned by the court on the basis of comparative blame. The manufacturer failed to test its product to ensure safety. And the distributor made safety claims to the public that were unfounded. An example of contributory negligence: a product was not fully tested by the manufacturer. However, the plaintiff used the product in an unsafe manner, ignoring a warning on the package. Thus, the court may rule that both the plaintiff and the defendant contributed to the loss. A judgment would be awarded only to the degree of the defendant's blame. See also *contributory negligence; negligence; tort law.*

compound interest   interest on interest, the time value of money. A sum of money left on deposit (or, a series of deposits over time) will grow in value as interest is credited. In subsequent periods, an ever increasing fund will be subject to a higher dollar amount of interest. For example, $5,000 is placed on deposit, with interest of 8% compounded quarterly (meaning that 2% will be added to the balance every three months). After one year, the value of the deposit is $5,412.16. See also *accumulated value; interest; principal; time value of money.* See illustration, page 36.

Comprehensive General Liability (CGL)   protection against all possible exposures to liability, less specifically named exclusions. Such policies are purchased by business concerns for product liability insurance, bodily injury protection for a range of environments, errors and omissions, and other possible losses. See also *bodily injury liability coverage; general liability; liability insurance; property and casualty insurance.*

comprehensive insurance   insurance that covers two or more different forms of loss. Individuals may purchase health insurance combining basic

compound interest

	QUARTERLY COMPOUNDING 8% PER YEAR	
MONTH	INTEREST	BALANCE
		$5,000.00
Mar	$100.00	5,100.00
Jun	102.00	5,202.00
Sep	104.04	5,306.04
Dec	106.12	5,412.16

hospital and major medical plans. Businesses may purchase comprehensive liability plans such as Special Multiperil Insurance (SMI). And comprehensive personal liability policies insure against all negligent acts but named exclusions. See also *health insurance; liability insurance; Special Multiperil Insurance (SMI).*

comprehensive liability protection within an automobile policy against property damage, theft, vandalism and other occurrences, with the exception of collision losses, which are covered separately. See also *automobile insurance.*

comprehensive major medical a health insurance policy that includes hospitalization and major medical protection, including coinsurance features and specified maximum benefits. See also *health insurance; major medical.*

comprehensive policy the most expensive form of homeowner's insurance, and the one providing the greatest extent of protection. Also called HO-5, it provides insurance for all risks except specifically named exclusions. See also *casualty insurance; HO-5; homeowner's insurance; liability insurance.*

condition concurrent a provision included in a contract stating that two separate events must occur at the same time. This may relate to performance requirements (such as payment of a premium in exchange for immediate effectiveness of coverage). See also *contract.*

condition precedent a provision in a contract stating that one event or action must occur before another may take place. For example, a policy may specify that insurance coverage cannot commence until the premium has been paid. See also *contract.*

condition subsequent a provision in a contract stating an event or action cannot take place until a previous event or action has been completed. For example, the contract may state that another person can be included in coverage only after the company has been notified in writing. Failing to do so will disqualify the second person from coverage in the event of a loss. See also *contract.*

conditional receipt a receipt given to create a contract on a temporary basis. Also called a conditional binding receipt, it establishes an insurance contract and coverage, effective at once. However, that contract is contingent upon approval by the underwriting department, successful completion of a medical examination, or other conditions. If the company rejects the application, the temporary contract is null and void. However, if the applicant is qualified and a loss occurs before final approval, the claim is valid. See also *binding receipt; contract; deposit premium.*

condominium policy a specialized form of homeowner's insurance designed for owners of condominium units, also called HO-6. It provides all-risk coverage on personal property and the unit itself, but not on the building or grounds owned as common elements with other homeowners. See also *casualty insurance; HO-6; homeowner's insurance; liability insurance.*

consequential loss any form of loss covered under an insurance policy, but not directly attributed to the casualty. For example, a fire destroys a home. The insurance policy will pay for replacement of the property. In addition, the family was forced to live in a hotel. Their loss of income for the hotel bill is a consequential loss. In business insurance, consequential losses include replacement of income a company is unable to earn following a casualty. See also *loss; risk.*

consideration **(1)** an element that must be present in order for a contract to be binding and legal. Consideration must be equal. For example, an insurance company accepts a risk as consideration for premium payments. (2) generally used to mean the premium paid by the insured, as consideration in an insurance or annuity contract. See also *contract; premium.*

constructive total loss a loss that is extensive enough to be considered total. Even when property may be partially recoverable, the cost of recovery or restoration may exceed current market value. See also *abandonment clause; total loss.*

Consumer Credit Insurance Association (CCIA) an association whose members are insurance companies that write credit life or disability insurance. This form of coverage protects the lender. In the event of death or disability, the lender receives payments against the loan or the balance outstanding under the contract. See also *credit life.*

contestability the right of an insurer to deny coverage, make a contract void, or question the validity of a claim. As a rule, the insurer has a specified period of time in which to contest a policy because the applicant supplied incomplete or misleading information on an application. See also *fraudulent misrepresentation; incontestability.*

contingency reserve a special reserve set up by an insurer to cover future contingent losses. These may be for surplus deficiencies, operating or investment losses, for payment of guaranteed dividends, or for unusually high claims. See also *dividend; investment income; loss reserves; mortality rate; reserve.*

contingent annuity a specialized form of annuity that promises to begin payments at a future date, in the event a specified event occurs. A survivorship annuity may be designed, for example, so that a surviving spouse will begin receiving payments when his or her spouse dies. See also *annuity; joint life and survivors annuity; survivorship annuity.*

---

contingent annuity

contingency

ACCUMULATION PERIOD   **PAYMENTS**

contingent beneficiary   a beneficiary who will receive benefits under a policy only if the primary beneficiary is no longer living when the insured person dies. See also *beneficiary; life insurance; primary beneficiary.*

contingent liability   a liability that might or might not come to be. For example, at the time an insurance company files its annual statement, it reports two forms of contingent liabilities. One is for a claim that the company is contesting; it might win, lose or settle. The other is for a lawsuit that has been filed against the company; they might win, lose or compromise in the future. Unreported claims are also considered a special form of contingent liability to insurers. See also *liability; unreported claim.*

continuous disability   a form of disability that does not disappear in time. See also *disability; partial disability; permanent total disability; total disability.*

contract   an agreement containing the elements of offer and acceptance, and consideration, entered into by legally competent individuals or companies. See also *acceptance; capacity; consideration; offer.*

contract of insurance   a unilateral agreement between the insurer and the insured. The insurer accepts a risk in return for premium payments by the insured. In the event of a loss, the company will reimburse the insured or pay damages directly. See also *insurance contract; policy; unilateral contract.*

contributory negligence   a concept in tort law stating that an individual might be partially responsible for his or her losses. This is distinguished from comparative negligence, which is a form of blame shared by two or more defendants. An example of contributory negligence: a tenant sues a landlord for property damages resulting from a leaky roof. However, the tenant failed to notify the landlord for several days after the damage was discovered; as a result, the loss was more extensive than it would have been if corrected immediately. Both the landlord and tenant contributed to the loss, and the court may assign contributory blame. The plaintiff's award will be limited to an estimate of damages recoverable if the damage had been reported at the time it was discovered. An example of comparative negligence: a tenant sues both the landlord and a roofing company for damages caused by a leaky roof. The roofer failed to install the roof properly, leading to the damage. However, the landlord was responsible for inspecting the property and did not do so. In addition, the landlord did not respond when advised of the condition. The judgment may be assigned to each defendant on the basis of comparative negligence. See also *comparative negligence; negligence; tort law.*

convention blank   industry term for the annual statement filed by insurance companies with the Commissioner of Insurance. The format is uniform in all states. See also *annual statement; Commissioner of Insurance; financial statement; National Association of Insurance Commissioners (NAIC).*

conventional method   statutory accounting procedures; methods of valuation used by insurance companies. Premiums, policy loan balances, and cash values are accounted for at current cash value only, without consideration for earned or accrued values applicable to future periods. For example, commissions paid during the first year exceed the premium receipts on the same policy. Under Generally Accepted Accounting Principles (GAAP) rules, part of that commission should apply to future years. But under the convention (statutory) method, it is considered an expense in the year cash is actually paid to the agent. Similar differences apply in the setting of reserve values, recognition of non-cash expenses and income, and other accounting issues. See also *cash value; GAAP requirements; Generally Accepted Accounting Principles (GAAP); policy loan; premium; statutory accounting.*

conversion   **(1)** the act of replacing an existing insurance policy with another one. For example, one policy allows the insured to exchange a term policy for a whole life policy of the same amount. No medical exam is required if the conversion option is exercised, although a different premium will be charged, based upon the permanent benefits of the whole life policy, and depending upon the current age of the insured. **(2)** in tort law, the wrongful acquiring, selling or using of property belonging to someone else, without the rightful owner's permission. See also *change of plan; convertible term; tort law.*

conversion factor   the assumed total fund required to satisfy the terms of an annuity, or to pay retirement benefits. The factor varies depending upon an assumed rate of interest, life expectancy, and the time between computation of present value and the normal retirement date. See also *actuarial present value; interest assumption; life expectancy; normal retirement age; present value.* See illustration, page 41.

conversion privilege   the right of an insured person to replace one policy with another. The privilege includes certain rights. For example, when an employee replaces group coverage with an individual version of the same policy, he is granted one month's grace period to make that decision and pay the initial premium; the company cannot refuse coverage. When a policyowner converts from term to whole life, the privilege usually includes

conversion factor

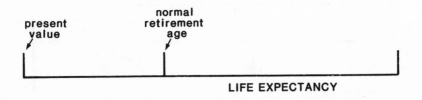

a stipulation that no medical exam or further evidence of insurability will be required. See also *change of plan; contract; evidence of insurability.*

convertible term   a form of term insurance that can, at the insured's option, be converted to another plan of insurance offered by the company. Most contracts allow the conversion without evidence of insurability. In making this a part of the contract, the company assumes the risk of adverse selection (the tendency of individuals to be more likely to keep insurance in force or to seek insurance when they are aware of their own poor health). See also *adverse selection; evidence of insurability; permanent life; term life.*

Coordination of Benefits (COB)   a provision designed by the Health Insurance Association of America (HIAA) and included in group health policies, restricting the payment of benefits when two or more policies overlap. The purpose of this provision is to limit benefit payments to 100%. See also *group health; Health Insurance Association of America (HIAA).*

co-payment   the percentage of covered expenses in a health insurance or Medicare program, for which the insured must pay. For example, a policy states that, after the deductible, the company will reimburse 80% of covered charges, to a stated maximum benefit. The remaining 20% is the co-payment portion. See also *coinsurance; covered expenses; health insurance; Medicare.* See illustration, page 42.

Cost of Living Adjustment (COLA)   a rider available with certain forms of insurance, providing that benefits will be modified to correspond with changes in the Consumer Price Index. This provision is found in disability, property and casualty and homeowner's policies, and is also built into the Social Security retirement calculation. See also *disability income; homeowner's insurance; property and casualty insurance; rider.*

co-payment

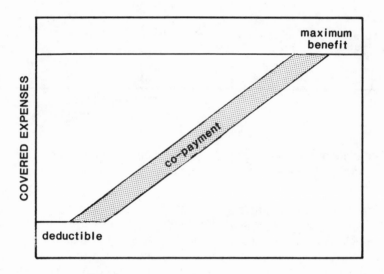

coupon plan a form of life insurance in which the policyowner clips and submits a series of coupons, and receives a "dividend" in return. This is not a dividend in the true sense, which would be a share of profits in a participating policy. Rather, the coupon payment is a partial return of premium. See also *guaranteed dividend; life insurance.*

coverage the extent of protection given to the insured by terms of the contract. See also *contract; loss.*

covered expenses in a health or liability insurance policy, those expenses eligible for reimbursement or payment by the insurer. The company will pay all covered expenses in excess of a deductible and coinsurance portion. See also *coinsurance; deductible; health insurance; property and casualty insurance.*

credit life a form of decreasing term life insurance on the life of a borrower. The lender is named as beneficiary, and the insurance is kept in force for as long as the loan is outstanding. The benefit amount matches the loan's balance during the term. In the event of the insured's death, the lender is repaid by the insurance company. See also *decreasing term life; life insurance; term life.* See illustration, page 43.

credit life

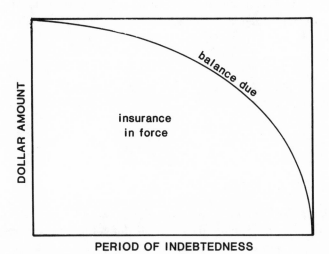

PERIOD OF INDEBTEDNESS

---

critical premium   the first premium due after payment of the initial premium on a new policy. It is considered critical because the majority of lapses occur after payment of the first premium. See also *initial premium; lapse; premium.*

crude death rate   total deaths during a period of time, expressed as a ratio to total population. See also *death rate; mortality rate.*

cumulative liability   **(1)** the total limitation an insurance company places on all policies on a single risk, to include directly carried and ceded risks. **(2)** the total limit of risk an insurer will allow on a single risk for all forms of liability insurance. See also *liability insurance; reinsurance; risk selection.*

cumulative trauma   a form of personal injury that extends beyond the immediate physical harm suffered. Health insurance policies may include provisions for payment of benefits for cumulative trauma, including psychic and indirect physical forms of loss. See also *health insurance; personal injury.*

current assumptions   a method of estimating premium, benefit and reserve levels based on mortality rates and interest assumptions about the future, rather than basing such estimates on historical information. For example, an actuary concludes that future investment income will be lower than it was in the past, due to changing market conditions. This affects the amount of premium to be charged on policies, and the amount to be established in a claims reserve. See also *benefit; interest assumption; life insurance; mortality; premium.*

curtesy the rights accruing to a widower in his wife's estate. See also *dower; elective share.*

D

date of issue the date of an insurance policy, when an application is approved. The actual effective date can be different. For example, an individual requests insurance effective as of February 1. The date of issue is February 10, but coverage was in effect as of the requested date. See also *effective date; issue.*

death benefit the amount to be paid to a beneficiary upon the death of the insured person, also called the policy's face amount. See also *benefit; face amount; life insurance.*

death rate the calculated probability of the number of deaths that will occur, on average, at a specified age. See also *mortality rate; probability.*

debit insurance a form of life insurance, also known as industrial insurance, on which premiums are collected on a weekly or monthly basis, often in person. The face amount is generally small. See also *face amount; industrial life; life insurance.*

declaration a statement made in an application for insurance. Policies are issued on the basis of declarations, including decisions about assigning special rates for certain risks. See also *loss, premium; rated policy; underwriting.*

declination the right of an insurer to reject an application for insurance, based on medical reasons or certain types of risk, such as the individual's occupation or recreational pursuits. See also *life insurance; medical examination; uninsurable risk.*

decreasing term life   a form of life insurance in which the premium remains level for a specified number of years (the term). However, the face amount of insurance declines during that term. See also *face amount; level term; life insurance.*

---

decreasing term life

insurance in force

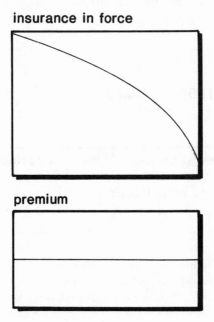

premium

---

deductible   (1) the amount of a loss that is excluded at the time of payment. Also called coinsurance, the insured is expected to assume a part of the total risk. In most policies, the deductible should be considered a form of partial self-insurance. The deductible is either a stated dollar amount or a percentage of the total, or a combination of both. For example, a policy specifies that it will pay 80% of claims to a maximum of $1 million. The deductible portion is 20% of all claims to the maximum; and all claims above the maximum. (2) a specified amount of time, also called the elimination period, during which an individual is not insured, or must wait before claims will accrue. In some forms of group insurance, a newly hired employee cannot be covered until the elimination period has passed. Disability insurance policies often specify that, upon becoming disabled, the insured cannot begin to receive benefits until a number of days (commonly 30) has passed. See also *benefit; coinsurance; elimination period; self-insurance.*

deferred annuity   a form of annuity in which the premiums are paid currently, but benefits are scheduled to begin at a later date. Premiums can be paid as a series of installments or as a single lump sum. Annuitization begins after a specified number of years, or in the year a specified age is attained. See also *annuity; benefit period; installment deferred annuity; single premium deferred annuity.*

deferred annuity

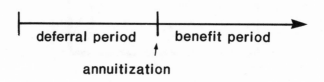

deferral period   benefit period

annuitization

deferred compensation plan   an arrangement in which a portion of an employee's compensation is withheld, to be paid at a later date. Income taxes on the deferred portion are also deferred, usually until retirement. The plan provides tax deferral benefits and retirement income to the employee, and reduces the chances that key employees will move to other companies. In order to qualify for the deferral provision, the deferral agreement must be made before income is earned. See also *retirement plan; tax deferral.*

deferred contribution plan   a type of plan in which payments to an employee's profit sharing plan are made on a deferred basis. For example, the maximum allowed contribution in one year is 15%. In one year, a 10% contribution is made. The following year, the employer is allowed to deduct a 15% contribution, plus the carried-over 5% credit from the year before. See also *profit sharing plan; tax deferral.*

deferred group annuity   an annuity in which the collective contributions made for the entire group are used each year to purchase paid-up deferred annuities. Upon retirement, each participant in the group receives a proportionate share of benefits. See also *annuity; group annuity; paid-up addition; pure annuity; refund annuity.*

deferred premium   that portion of premium that has been paid, but is not yet due. For example, a policyholder pays premium on an annual basis. In the first month, 1/12th of the total is due, and the remainder is deferred. Deferred premium payments can be made on an annual, semiannual or quarterly mode. See also *anniversary date; modal premium; policy anniversary; premium.*

---

deferred premium

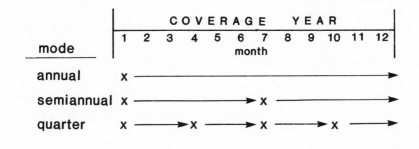

deferred vesting   a method of crediting benefits to participants in a pension plan or profit sharing plan over a period of months or years. See also *pension plan; profit sharing plan; vesting.*

deficiency reserve   an additional reserve that an insurance company must establish, when the gross premium is lower than the net premium (deficient). The reserve must be maintained until the deficiency is absorbed. See also *gross premium; life insurance; net premium; reserve.*

defined benefit plan   a pension plan in which the benefits are determined by formula, and contributions are adjusted each year to meet the future requirement. See also *pension plan; retirement plan.*

defined contribution plan   also called a money purchase plan, a form of pension plan in which the amount of annual contribution is fixed as a percentage of each employee's salary or another formula. See also *money purchase plan; pension plan; retirement plan.*

delay clause a provision in whole life insurance policies allowing the insurer to delay granting a policy loan for a period up to six months, except for the purpose of paying current premiums. See also *cash value; policy loan; whole life insurance.*

delayed payment a common disaster clause, in which payment of a death benefit may be withheld by the insurance company for a stated period of time. In the event the primary beneficiary does not survive this period, benefits will be paid to a contingent beneficiary. For example, a husband and wife are involved in an accident. The husband dies, and the wife is in critical condition. If she does not survive, the provision can be put into effect. See also *common disaster clause; death benefit; life insurance.*

delivery the acknowledgment of liability on the part of an insurance company. Delivery is achieved when the insurer accepts a conditional receipt, or upon advising the insured that a policy is in effect. See also *binding receipt; conditional receipt; contract; initial premium.*

dependency period the years during which a family has dependent children under the age of 18. During this period, surviving spouses are eligible for Social Security benefits. See also *life insurance; Social Security Act of 1935.*

dependent an individual who depends on the insured person for support, including spouses and unmarried children or step-children. See also *beneficiary; insurable interest.*

dependent insurance forms of coverage under life or health insurance policies that extend to the insured person's dependents. See also *coverage; health insurance; life insurance.*

deposit administration group annuity a form of group annuity in which members of a group make periodic contributions (or contributions are made by an employer in their behalf), to a single fund. These contributions are made during the accumulation period, with payments beginning at a later date (the benefit period). Proportionate shares of benefits are made to each member. See also *accumulation benefits; annuity; benefit period; group annuity.* See illustration, page 49.

deposit administration group annuity

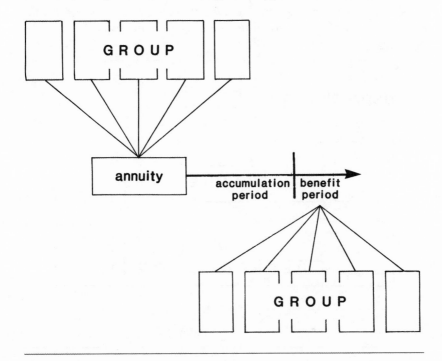

deposit premium   a provisional premium required under the terms of insurance policies subject to experience modification. An adjustment is made at the end of a policy year, based on actual claims filed, or upon determination of exposure to losses. See also *adjustable premium; experience modification; exposure to loss; initial premium.*

deposit term life   a form of life insurance in which a deposit is paid at the beginning of the first year, and left with the insurance company for a number of years. In the event the policy is lapsed, all or part of the deposit is forfeited; otherwise, it is returned with interest at the end of the specified period. The purpose of the deposit is to encourage policyholders to keep policies in force long enough for the insurance company to recover its expenses during the first year, which often exceed premium income. See also *forfeiture; lapse; retention; term life.*

depreciation   the calculated or actual deterioration in value of property. Depreciation is calculated for the purpose of determining the amount to be paid in property and casualty policies on the Actual Cash Value (ACV) basis—original cost minus annual depreciation. See also *Actual Cash Value (ACV); property and casualty insurance; replacement cost.*

depreciation

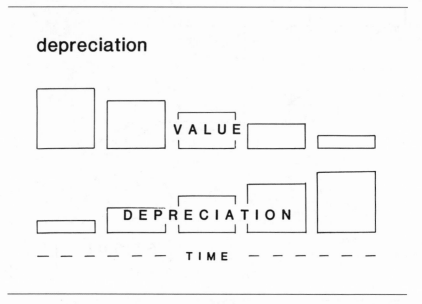

direct liability   the liability of an individual for losses incurred, as the result of negligence or intentional damages. See also *liability; negligence; property and casualty insurance.*

direct loss   a loss resulting specifically from an insured peril. All losses created by a chain of events stemming from that peril are direct losses. The distinction is one of proximate cause. The secondary effects of a casualty, or indirect losses, are excluded in casualty policies. See also *indirect loss; loss; property and casualty insurance.*

direct writer   a property and casualty insurer that writes insurance directly, through its employees or agency system. An indirect insurer sells through independent agents, brokers, reinsurers, or a combination of these other outlets. See also *broker; independent agent; property and casualty insurance; reinsurance.* See illustration, page 51.

direct writer

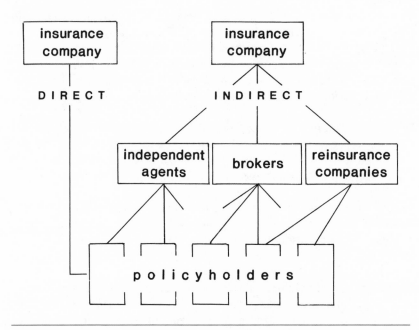

---

disability   an impairment or handicap resulting from accident or ill health, that prevents an individual from earning a living. In most policies, disability is defined as the inability to work at one's own occupation or an occupation for which the person is reasonably suited, by way of education or experience. A disability can be partial or total, and policies may extend coverage only in the case of a permanent disability. See also *partial disability; permanent partial disability; permanent total disability; total disability.*

disability benefit   **(1)** payments available to an insured person under a disability insurance policy. This benefit is normally paid either as a specified amount per month, or as a percentage of the insured's income, subject to limitations in (a) amount, and (b) the duration of payments. **(2)** a clause in many life insurance policies specifying that, in the event of total disability, insurance will remain in force but no continuing premiums will be required. See also *benefit; life insurance; Waiver of Premium (WP).*

disability buy-out   a form of insurance purchased by partnerships and corporations. In the event of disability of a partner or key employee, insurance benefits enable the other partners or stockholders to purchase the disabled person's interests. See also *buy-sell agreement.*

disability income the amount paid by an insurance company to a disabled policyholder. The payment is subject to limits. First, an elimination period must pass, during which benefits will not be paid. Second, the benefit is limited in amount and duration by policy provision. See also *elimination period; health insurance; income replacement; recurring disability clause; residual disability.*

Disability Insurance Training Council (DITC) an organization that provides insurance professionals with continuing education services. Primarily concerned with health insurance, the Council was formed by the International Accident and Health Association. See also *health insurance.*

disability premium waiver a clause in a life insurance contract providing that, in the event of disability, the policy will remain in force but premium payments will be suspended. See also *life insurance; rider; Waiver of Premium (WP).*

disappearing deductible a provision in certain property and casualty policies, stipulating that after a deductible has been paid, the company will reimburse more than 100% of losses incurred. This offset continues until the original deductible has been absorbed. See also *deductible; property and casualty insurance.* See illustration, page 53.

discount a reduction from a full charge, or the present value of a future sum. A discounted present value will accumulate to the desired sum, assuming a principal amount or a series of payments; an interest rate; and the amount of time involved. See also *accumulated value; interest; mortality; present value.*

discounted premium any premium paid to an insurance company in advance of the period to which it applies. See also *advance premium; premium.*

discovery period the time during which information covered under an insurance policy must be reported. A surety company, for example, will specify that upon termination of a bond, the principal must report any claimed losses within the discovery period. See also *bond; loss; surety bond.*

discrimination the favoring of one group over another, or failing to provide services or benefits on an equal footing on the basis of a group's

disappearing deductible

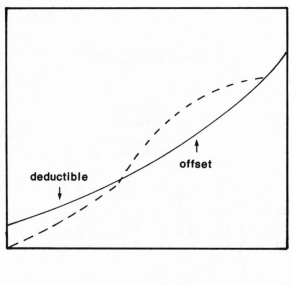

deductible

offset

————— **losses**

distinction. Discrimination may occur in profit sharing and pension plans, when higher compensated officers, shareholders or employees receive greater benefits than lower paid employees. Insurance discrimination can occur geographically, by age, or by race. Example: an underwriter determines that mortality experience is greater for a specific race, or for people in one area. Accordingly, policies submitted by those groups are rejected. See also *rate discrimination; risk selection; underwriting.*

dismemberment benefit   health insurance that pays an insured in the event of the loss of one or more limbs or the sight in one or both eyes. See also *accidental death and dismemberment; health insurance.*

diversification   the spreading of risk over a large number of possible exposures. This is a basic concept of insurance. One individual cannot afford a catastrophic loss. However, when a large group contributes premiums, the small number who actually experience losses are reimbursed by the insurer. The larger the insured group, the greater the insurance company's diversification. The same principle applies to management of investment funds. See also *law of large numbers; risk selection.*

---

diversification

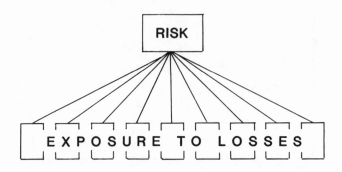

---

dividend a return of capital. Participating life insurance policies include a provision that the insured individual will receive dividends representing the insurance company's surplus after payment of claims. Some forms of participating policies include dividends based on actual mortality experience or operating net profits. Insurance dividends are not considered taxable income, but a partial return of premium. See also *life insurance; participating policy.*

dividend accumulation one of several options a participating life insurance policyowner can select. In this option, dividends are left with the insurance company to accumulate at interest. See also *accumulated dividends; compound interest.*

dividend addition one of several options a participating life insurance policyowner can select. In this option, dividends are applied to the purchase of fully paid-up additions of whole life insurance. See also *life insurance; paid-up addition; participating policy.*

dividend options choices that are made by policyowners in participating life insurance policies. Dividends earned can be applied in one of five ways:

1. To reduce premiums on continuing insurance coverage.
2. Paid to the policyowner in cash.
3. To purchase paid-up additions of whole-life insurance.
4. Left on deposit to accumulate at compound interest.
5. Applied to the purchase of extended term insurance, usually for one-year periods.
See also *paid-up addition; participating policy.*

---

dividend options

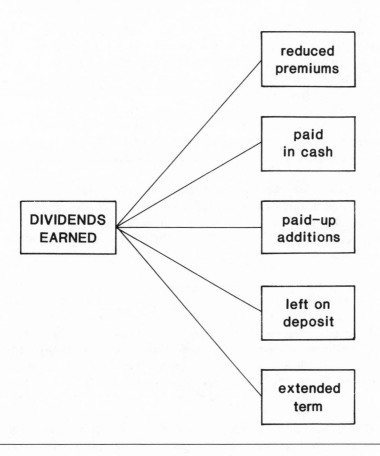

---

dividend rate the interest rate paid by an insurance company to policy-owners in participating policies. This rate is used to calculate the amount of dividend earned. See also *interest rate; participating policy.*

divisible surplus the amount available for payment of dividends to participating policyowners. It represents the company's surplus after payment of claims. See also *life insurance; participating policy.*

domestic company an insurance company that is incorporated and located in a specific state. See also *foreign company; insurer.*

double indemnity a provision in many life insurance contracts, specifying that in the event of accidental death, double the face amount will be paid to the beneficiary. See also *accidental death; face amount; life insurance.*

double recovery a condition in which an insured person or company would receive benefits in excess of covered amounts, as a result of carrying two or more insurance policies. In such cases, the practice of Coordination of Benefits (COB) prevents policyholders from receiving more than 100% of claimed losses. See also *Coordination of Benefits (COB); loss settlement.*

dower the proportionate right of a widow to receive a share of her husband's estate, also called elective share. See also *curtesy; elective share.*

Drive Other Car endorsement (DOC) provision in an automobile insurance policy, providing coverage when a loss occurs while driving in a vehicle other than the one covered by the policy. Separate DOC endorsements must be obtained for business and for personal losses. See also *automobile insurance.*

dry trust a trust in which there is no required action on the part of the trustee. See also *trust.*

dual capacity descriptive of liability that might exist in two or more ways. One individual or company can have dual capacity, and claimed losses might apply under any relationship. Example: An employee works in her employer's home. The employer/homeowner may be liable in the capacity of employer, and also in the capacity of homeowner. See also *liability.*

duplicated benefits condition in health insurance policies when an insured is covered for one loss under two separate policies. The policy of Coordination of Benefits (COB) is applied, designating one insurer as a primary carrier, and the other as secondary. Each is then responsible for a proportionate share of the total claim. See also *benefit; Coordination of Benefits (COB); health insurance.* See illustration, page 57.

duplicated benefits

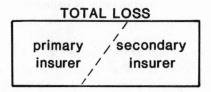

TOTAL LOSS

| primary insurer | secondary insurer |

E

earned premium   that portion of premium received by an insurance company and earned in the current month. The excess is deferred as unearned, until a future date. See also *premium; unearned premium.*

---

earned premium

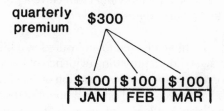

quarterly premium $300

| $100 | $100 | $100 |
| JAN | FEB | MAR |

---

earning limitation   a provision in Social Security rules specifying that, in order to receive the maximum old age benefits allowed, the individual may not earn more than a specified amount of other income. When that limit is exceeded, Social Security benefits are reduced by one dollar for every two dollars of additional income earned. See also *Social Security Act of 1935.*

economic life value   a computed estimate of the earning potential of an individual, for the purpose of determining the appropriate amount of disability income or life insurance required. The purpose is to determine the potential loss in the event that earning potential is halted due to disability or premature death. See also *disability income; life insurance.*

economic value   the current value of property. In a property and casualty insurance policy, economic value describes replacement cost, net of depreciation. See also *property and casualty insurance; replacement cost.*

education endowment   an endowment policy held for the purpose of providing for the future cost of a child's education. The maturity date is set as of a child's age, or a specified number of years from the date the policy commences. See also *endowment; maturity date.*

effective date   the date that coverage begins under the terms of an insurance policy. This date might not be identical to the date of issue. The effective date can precede the issue date, or can be delayed. See also *date of issue.*

elective indemnity   a clause in some disability income policies, giving the insured person a choice of receiving a lump sum distribution instead of regular monthly payments. The clause might specify that the elective indemnity provision applies for only certain types of injuries. See also *disability income; indemnity; lump sum distribution.*

elective share   the right of an individual to receive a portion of a deceased spouse's net estate. See also *curtesy; dower.*

eligibility period   the time allowed to an insured in a life or health policy, to enroll for coverage without providing evidence of insurability, usually by way of a medical examination. Upon expiration of the eligibility period, that evidence might be required, based on the amount of insurance and the applicant's age. See also *evidence of insurability; health insurance; life insurance.*

eligibility requirements   the specific rules set forth in a pension plan that determine whether or not an employee may participate in that plan. The formula involves years of service, hours worked per year, or a combination of both. See also *pension plan.*

eligible employee   an employee who meets the requirements for participation in a company-sponsored retirement plan. For example, the plan specifies that only full-time employees may qualify, and defines full-time as any individual who works more than a specified number of hours per month. See also *retirement plan.*

elimination period   a waiting period during which the insured person is either not covered by the plan (health insurance), or must wait before beginning to receive benefits (disability income policy). See also *deductible; disability income; health insurance.*

employee   for the purpose of determining eligibility to obtain coverage under a group insurance policy or pension or profit sharing plan, an individual who works for an employer and is under that employer's control. The definition includes location where work is performed, degree of supervision, and the number of hours committed to the job. See also *group contract; pension plan; profit sharing plan.*

employee contribution   an amount of money deducted from an employee's paycheck and deposited into a group contract or company retirement plan. This may consist of an employee's share of the total cost, or a voluntary additional contribution. See also *group contract; retirement plan.*

Employee Retirement Income Security Act (ERISA)   also known as the Pension Reform Act of 1974, a federal law establishing limitations on annual contributions to pension and profit sharing plans, and setting standards for determining contribution formulas. See also *pension plan; profit sharing plan; tax deferral.*

Employee Stock Ownership Plan (ESOP)   a retirement plan designed to enable owners to transfer a company's equity to employees, under a tax-deferred procedure. Contributions are made for employees by way of the purchase of company stock. Plans can also include life insurance benefits to participants. ESOP's ensure continuity of business after the retirement of the present owner, increase employee motivation as part owners, and provide retirement value. See also *life insurance; qualified plan; retirement plan.*

Employee Stock Ownership Trust (ESOT)   a trust formed primarily to borrow funds that will be paid by an ESOP. For example, a present owner wants to retire and transfer ownership through establishment of an ESOP. However, a complete transfer will require many years, and the owner wants a cash sum today. By establishing an ESOT, the funds are borrowed and paid to the retiring owner. See also *trust.*

endorsement   a modifying provision added to an existing insurance contract, either to increase coverage or to add restrictions to eligible losses. See also *policy; rider.*

endowment   a form of life insurance in which the full face value will be paid to the policyowner upon reaching a specified maturity date. Between the time the endowment contract is formed and the maturity date, the insured person is fully covered for the face amount. In the event of death, that amount will be paid to the beneficiary. See also *face amount; life insurance; maturity date.*

entire contract clause   a statement in a life or health insurance contract stating that the application and the policy constitute the entire contract between the company and the insured. See also *contract; health insurance; life insurance.*

entity plan   a form of buy-sell agreement designed to enable stockholders or partners to purchase the interests of another, in the event of death or disability. See also *buy-sell agreement; disability buy-out; key employee insurance.*

equity   **(1)** the equal treatment of all individuals in a common plan. For example, an insurance company cannot set rates based on discriminatory premises. **(2)** the net worth of a person or company, computed by subtracting liabilities from assets. See also *discrimination; net worth; risk selection.*

equity linked   descriptive of variable life insurance policies, in which the equity in the policy changes on the basis of current market values. See also *life insurance; variable life.*

estate planning   the anticipation of expenses related to distributing wealth following death, and for providing replacement of economic losses. An estate plan allows for estate and inheritance taxes, the needs of surviving dependents, payment of debts, and provision of assets to beneficiaries. See also *financial plan; life insurance; tax planning.*

estate tax   a tax assessed by the federal government on the value of assets of a deceased individual. See also *inheritance tax; tax planning.*

estimated premium   a premium charged at the beginning of a period, but subject to adjustments at a later date. The adjustment will be based on actual losses experienced by the company, a procedure known as retrospective rating. See also *experience modification; premium; retrospective rating.*

evidence clause   a contractual clause in which the insured person agrees to provide all evidence requested by the company to prove the amount of occurrence of a claim. See also *claim; contract; settlement.*

evidence of insurability   proof given by an applicant for insurance, that the individual is in good health. The purpose is to verify statements made on an application, or to reduce risks to the insurer of undiscovered conditions. Evidence may be required based on the applicant's age, amount or type of insurance, or both. See also *adverse selection; eligibility period; health insurance; life insurance; medical examination.*

exact interest   interest computed on a daily compounded rate, assuming 365 days in the year (as opposed to the alternative daily compounding method, using 360 days). See also *compound interest; interest rate.*

exact interest

$$\frac{\text{annual rate}}{\text{365 days}} = \text{daily rate}$$

$$\frac{8.5\%}{365} = .0002328$$

excess contribution   an amount paid into a qualified retirement plan that is greater than the maximum allowed per employee. The excess is subject to an additional penalty or excise tax, depending on the type of plan. See also *qualified plan; retirement plan.*

excess insurance   coverage provided in an insurance plan above a primary or initial range of losses. In health insurance plans, for example, the insurer's liability will extend to a primary range at a stated percentage of the total; and then extend in an excess range (often to a maximum of $1 million). See also *coverage; loss.*

excess interest   an amount of interest paid to a policyowner in a life insurance contract, above a guaranteed rate of interest. For example, a company guarantees that it will pay 3% per year; during the first year, the actual rate—based on profits investment income and loss experience—is paid out at 7%. See also *cash value; guaranteed rate of interest; interest; life insurance.*

excess of loss plan   a schedule for the method of paying losses, commonly found in reinsurance agreements. Rather than applying ceded limits to a range of policies, a maximum loss will be paid on each claim or each policy, to a specified limit above an identified loss level. See also *ceding company; loss; reinsurance ceded.*

excess policy   an insurance policy that is designed to reimburse losses above the limits provided in a separate policy, or when another policy's term expires. See also *loss; umbrella policy.*

exclusion   the types of losses or risks that a policy does not cover. Some exclusions are standard, such as the life insurance exclusion for suicide during the first two years the policy is in force, or death from acts of war. Other risks are excluded as additions. For example, an individual reveals on an application for health insurance a history of eye problems. The policy is issued with the stipulation that coverage for eye problems is not covered. See also *coverage; pre-existing condition.*

exclusion ratio   the computation of income from an annuity contract, with the distinction made that one part is excluded from tax, representing a return of premium; and another portion represents taxable income. See also *annuity; tax deferral.* See illustration, page 63.

exclusive agency   an arrangement between an insurer and an agency, stipulating that the agency will sell a specific line of insurance products written only by that company. Some forms of exclusive agency extend to a limited group of insurers offering the same product, or lines of products. In comparison, an independent agency agreement allows the agency to represent many different insurance carriers. See also *agent; captive agent; independent agent.* See illustration, page 63.

exclusion ratio

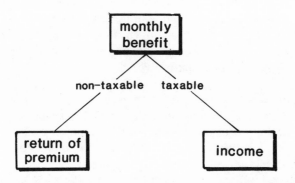

exclusive agency

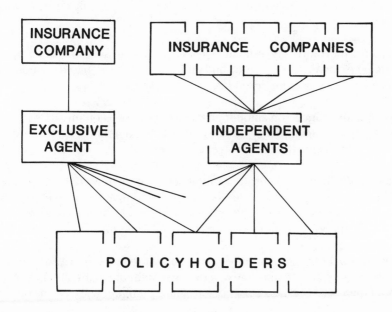

exculpatory clause a provision that releases an insurer from loss liability in the event that a loss occurs due to negligence or omissions of the insured. See also *contract; negligence.*

executor the individual charged with the fiduciary duty to dispose of or execute the will of a deceased person. The testator's preference of executors may be stated in a will, although actual appointment can be made by a court. See also *fiduciary; testator; will.*

exhaust loan a policy loan granted in an amount that completely uses up the current cash value, when premium and loan repayments are not made within the 30-day grace period. As a result, the policy lapses, or expires. See also *cash value ; expiration; lapse; life insurance; policy loan.*

exhibit a page in the annual statement (convention blank), an extensive financial report filed by insurance companies with their state commissioners of insurance. See also *annual statement; Commissioner of Insurance; convention blank.*

expected morbidity the estimated level of claims an insurance company expects to have during a year and for a specific age group, based on statistical averages listed on a morbidity table. See also *health insurance; morbidity.*

expected mortality the estimated level of deaths a life insurance company anticipates for a given age group and during a single year, based on mortality table rates. See also *life insurance; mortality.*

expense allowance an amount paid to agents above commissions earned, incurred in the selling of insurance policies. The amount is agreed upon in advance by contract. See also *agent; commission.*

expense constant a recurring amount added to the premium of insurance policies to provide for expenses the insurance company will (a) experience every year the policy is in force, or (b) absorbs once and then recovers over the time the policy is in force. See also *load; premium.*

expense load the amount added to insurance premiums to pay for commissions, general and administrative expenses, premium taxes, and marketing or selling costs. See also *commission; load; premium tax; rate making.*

expense ratio a ratio showing the relationship between incurred expenses connected to writing policies, and the amount of written premium. The ratio does not include claims. For example, during one month, a particular line of insurance has $355,100 in written premium, and the company incurs $54,800 in expenses. The expense ratio is 15.4%. See also *premium; written premium.*

---

expense ratio

$$\frac{\text{incurred expenses}}{\text{written premium}} = \text{expense ratio}$$

$$\frac{\$54,800}{\$355,100} = 15.4\%$$

---

expense reimbursement   money paid by life insurance companies to independent or captive agents for their general and administrative expenses, in addition to commissions. See also *agent; captive agent; life insurance.*

experience   actual losses an insurer has during a year or other period of time. See also *claim; incurred loss; loss.*

experience modification   an adjustment—either increase or decrease—in premiums based on the actual loss experience for a previous period of time. See also *retrospective rating.*

experience rate   the percentage applied to the cost of premiums in a subsequent period, based on the loss experience during the past period. The rate may be greater or less than the previous rate. For example, one insured company submitted claims 3.4% lower than the insurer anticipated. The experience rate for the following year was 96.4% (100% of prior premiums, less 3.4% experience rate). In the event that claims exceeded the amount the insurer anticipated, the experience rate would be above 100%. See also *loss; retrospective rating.*

experience refund   an alternative term describing the experience rate; a reduced premium in a subsequent period based on lower claims than expected; or, an actual refund paid by a reinsurer to the ceding company for a favorable loss experience. See also *adjustable premium; premium; retrospective rating.*

---

experience refund

$$\frac{\text{actual losses}}{\text{expected losses}} = \text{experience}$$

$$\frac{\$625,815}{\$685,000} = 91.36\%$$

---

experienced morbidity   the actual level of claims submitted to a health insurance company during a year, compared to the expected morbidity. See also *health insurance; morbidity.*

experienced mortality   the actual level of death claims submitted to a life insurance company during a year, compared to expected mortality. See also *life insurance; mortality.*

expiration   the date a policy ceases to exist, when coverage ceases, often the anniversary date, the end of a specified term, or the renewal date (if the policy can be renewed or continued). See also *anniversary date; renewal term; termination.*

expiration notice   a notification sent by an insurance company when premiums are overdue, advising that the policy will terminate as of a specified date. See also *lapse; termination.*

expiry   the cessation of coverage under an insurance policy, at the end of an agreed upon term. Depending on the policy provisions, policies may be extended, converted, or renewed, often with the amount of premium to be renegotiated. See also *termination.*

exposure to loss   the contingency of loss that an insurance company assumes in several ways: By concentration in one geographic area, by writing of many policies on a similar form of loss, or by providing protection against a single loss to one company or individual. Exposure to loss can be mitigated by diversification, such as reinsuring that portion of coverage above retention limits. An individual or company is exposed to losses in not carrying insurance. In some instances, a particular loss can be fully or partially coinsured, or no insurance is carried, so that the person or company is self-insured. See also *coinsurance; diversification; loss; probability; reinsurance; retention; risk; self-insurance.*

express covenant   parts of contracts that exist due to specific statements, as opposed to implied warranties or promises commonly held to exist. See also *contract.*

extended coverage   an agreement between an insurance company and the insured, to provide additional protection in return for a higher premium. This coverage, usually provided by way of a rider, extends the scope of coverage in a policy. For example, the policyholder of an automobile insurance contract extends coverage by adding another person as a covered driver of a car. See also *coverage; endorsement; rider.*

extended term   insurance available as a nonforfeiture option in a life insurance policy. Cash value is applied to the purchase of extended term insurance. The amount and duration of coverage are determined by the total of cash value available, the amount of insurance purchased, and the age of the insured. See also *attained age; cash value; life insurance; nonforfeiture option; term life.*

extra dividend   a dividend paid to a policyholder above the amount of guaranteed dividend. See also *dividend; excess interest; guaranteed dividend.*

extra premium   the premium added to the regular premium when a policy is rated. This occurs when the insurance company determines the risk is greater of experiencing a loss. See also *premium; rated policy; substandard risk.*

F

face amount   the full benefit of a life insurance policy, also called the amount in force. In the event of the insured's death, the face amount is paid to the beneficiary. See also *in force; life insurance.*

face amount certificate   a contract specifying the total amount that will be paid in the future, such as the maturity value of an investment or annuity. See also *annuity; contract.*

factual expectation   the anticipation of future value that creates an insurable interest. For example, a father states that he will give his son the family car in one year. The son has a factual expectation that, in the event of damage to the car, he will lose the value of the asset; thus, he has an insurable interest in the car. See also *insurable interest.*

Fair Access to Insurance Requirements (FAIR)   a program operated by the Federal Insurance Administration (FIA), designed to provide property and casualty insurance in areas where insurers do not want to assume a total risk, due to environmental or economic circumstances. The FAIR program establishes the insurance policy and then cedes it to private insurance companies through a system known as stop loss reinsurance. See also *Federal Insurance Administration (FIA); property and casualty insurance; reinsurance; stop loss reinsurance.*

Fair Credit Reporting Act (FCRA)   a federal law that grants an applicant for insurance the right to be informed about information contained in a credit report. See also *application.*

family dependency period   the years when children are economically dependent on an individual. This period is identified to determine the amount of insurance a wage earner needs until children have grown. See also *dependency period; needs approach.*

family income policy   a form of life insurance combining a whole life policy with decreasing term coverage. If the insured dies during a specified period of years, monthly income payments are made to the beneficiary (this is the decreasing term portion of the policy); and upon expiration of that period, the face amount of the whole life portion will also be paid. Upon expiration of the specified period, the decreasing term coverage ends. If the insured dies following that date, the beneficiary is entitled to payment of the whole life policy's face amount. See also *decreasing term life; face amount; life insurance; rider; whole life insurance.*

---

family income policy

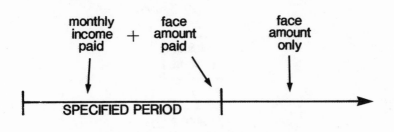

family maintenance policy life insurance containing both whole life and level term coverages. It may be established on terms similar to those in the family income policy; or may provide whole life on the principal wage earner and term on the lives of the spouse or the children. Upon expiration of the term period, the insured spouse or children often are granted the right to convert insurance to another plan. See also *conversion privilege; level term; life insurance; whole life insurance.*

family split dollar plan a method of payment when the insured cannot directly afford the full premium. Another family member pays a portion of the premiums and is given a collateral assignment. When cash value has been built up in the policy, the family member is reimbursed. See also *cash value; collateral assignment.* See illustration, page 70.

Federal Deposit Insurance Corporation (FDIC) a federal government agency that provides insurance up to $100,000 on every account kept in member banks. See also *risk; safety.*

Federal Employees Group Life Insurance (FEGLI) an insurance plan for federal employees. Insurance is provided through the FEGLI program, and the risk and income are reinsured to private insurance companies. See also *reinsurance.* See illustration, page 70.

family split dollar plan

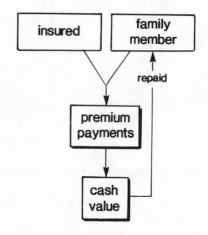

Federal Employees Group
Life Insurance (FEGLI)

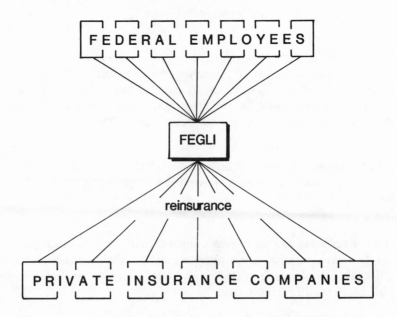

Federal Employees Liability Act (FELA) a federal law establishing insurance similar to each state's worker's compensation, but for federal employees. See also *accident and health; workers compensation.*

Federal Housing Administration (FHA) an agency of the federal government that assists individuals in buying homes, when they would not otherwise qualify for lenders' minimum risk standards. The FHA insures lenders against losses resulting from default. See also *mortgage insurance.*

Federal Insurance Administration (FIA) an agency of the federal government that administers several insurance programs, including the FAIR program. See also *Fair Access to Insurance Requirements (FAIR); reinsurance.*

Federal Insurance Contributions Act (FICA) legislation that established a payroll deduction to fund the Social Security program. See also *Social Security Act of 1935.*

Federal Savings and Loan Insurance Corporation (FSLIC) a federal government agency that provides insurance up to $100,000 on every account kept in member savings and loan associations. See also *risk; safety.*

Federal Security Agency (FSA) a federal agency that ensures compliance with Social Security and unemployment insurance regulations. See also *Social Security Act of 1935.*

Federal Trade Commission (FTC) a government commission that oversees—but does not directly regulate—the insurance agency. Regulation is conducted on the state level. See also *McCarren Act; National Association of Insurance Commissioners (NAIC).*

Fellow, Casualty Actuarial Society (FCAS) a member of the Casualty Actuarial Society (CAS) who has passed a series of examinations involving the casualty insurance industry. See also *actuary; Casualty Actuarial Society (CAS).*

Fellow, Institute of Actuaries (FIA) a designation awarded to qualified and tested actuaries. See also *actuary.*

Fellow, Life Management Institute (FLMI) a designation awarded to individuals who pass a series of examinations on a range of life and health insurance topics. See also *health insurance; life insurance; Life Management Institute (LMI).*

Fellow, Society of Actuaries (FSA) a designation awarded to individuals who successfully pass a series of examinations. See also *actuary; Society of Actuaries (SA).*

fidelity bond insurance against losses resulting from theft or dishonest acts of employees. The bond can identify named individuals or can apply to any employee of the insured. See also *bond; surety bond.*

fiduciary an individual responsible for the management of money or property in a trust, or as executor, administrator or adviser; one who represents another person in financial matters. See also *administrator; beneficiary; executor; trust.*

final insurance descriptive of premium payments made through borrowing cash value in a whole life policy. See also *cash value; whole life insurance.*

finance plan an agreement between an insurance company and a newly hired agent. The company agrees to compensate the agent at a specified level for a limited period of time. The agent is given goals for the development of new business, and agrees to reimburse the company when earnings exceed the advances. See also *agent; commission.*

finance plan

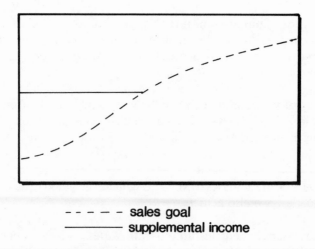

‑ ‑ ‑ ‑ ‑ **sales goal**
——— **supplemental income**

financial plan a written plan that anticipates and prepares for future financial needs, provides for known and unknown risks, and establishes the means to achieve identified personal financial goals. The complete plan will include identification of insurance and investment needs. See also *estate planning; retirement plan; tax planning.*

financial planner   an individual who offers financial planning services. While there is no state or national legislation or consistent standards for qualifying a financial planner, several professional designations indicate the individual has a scope of knowledge on financial matters. These include the CFP, CFA and ChFC designations. The term financial planner often is assumed by individuals who have only one product to sell, such as insurance or mutual funds. A comprehensive planning service should include the participation of several specialists, including experts in estate matters, investments, insurance, and taxation. See also *Certified Financial Planner (CFP); Chartered Financial Analyst (CFA); Chartered Financial Consultant (ChFC).*

financial statement   a summary of status or operations of a company. There are three types of financial statement:
   balance sheet—this summarizes the assets and liabilities of a company as of a specified date such as the end of the year. The difference between these two represents net worth.
   income statement—the results of operations for a specified period of time, usually one full year. Gross income is reduced by costs and expenses, with the balance representing net profits.
   cash flow statement—also called the sources and applications of funds statement, this shows the use of cash during a specified period, usually one year.
Financial statements are included in the annual statement filed by insurance companies. See also *annual statement; Commissioner of Insurance; convention blank.*

fire insurance   a form of coverage, also known as homeowner's insurance, that protects against the economic consequences of losses from fires, acts of God, theft, vandalism, theft, burglary, and other losses. A policy can provide limited coverage or a wide range of protection. Two forms of insurance are included: liability insurance protects homeowners against losses from injuries suffered by other people or damages to the property of others. Casualty insurance protects against losses to the homeowner's own property. The standard form fire insurance policy contains four parts:
> I—declarations (location of the property, the name of the insured, and the amount and type of insurance)
> II—insuring agreements (premium, actions of the insurance company

and the insured, and obligations
of both sides)
III—conditions (restrictions of coverage)
IV—exclusions (property or types of
losses that are not included)

See also *casualty insurance; homeowner's insurance; liability insurance; multiple perils; standard form.*

first party coverage the portion of a loss that is assigned to a reinsurer, when losses exceed the issuing company's retention limits. See also *reinsurance; retention.*

first surplus an agreement for prorated risks that are shared between the issuing company and a reinsurer. The prorated risks can either be fixed by amount or may vary by degree or type of risk. See also *reinsurance; surplus reinsurance.*

first year commission the commission an agent earns based on premiums paid by the insured during the first year. As an incentive to generate new business, agents are compensated at attractive first year rates. This commission often exceeds 100% of the premium received, with renewal commissions substantially lower. See also *commission; new business.*

Five Million Dollar Forum (FMDF) an organization formed to recognize agents who are responsible for placing five million dollars or more in new business. See also *life insurance.*

five percent rule a coinsurance clause in many property and casualty insurance policies, that when a loss is lower than a specified amount (often $10,000), and when that loss is lower than five percent of the total value of covered property, the insurance company will not require a detailed inventory or appraisal of the remaining property. See also *appraisal; coinsurance; property and casualty insurance.*

fixed amount option also called the fixed payment option, a settlement mode in many life insurance contracts, under which the death benefit is paid out to the beneficiary as a series of fixed-amount installments. The period over which payments will continue is determined by the amount of death benefit available. See also *life insurance optional settlement mode; settlement option.* See illustration, page 75.

fixed dollar annuity a form of annuity contract in which the amount of periodic payments is determined and fixed in advance. The contract will specify that this amount will continue to be paid for a number of years,

fixed amount option

$$\frac{\text{installments}}{\text{total proceeds}} = \text{time}$$

or for the remainder of the annuitant's life. See also *annuity; variable dollar annuity.*

fixed period option a settlement option under which the death benefit is retained by the insurance company, and periodic payments are made to the beneficiary for a specified number of years. The amount of each payment will be determined by the amount of death benefit available. See also *life insurance; optional settlement mode; settlement option.*

fixed period option

$$\frac{\text{time}}{\text{total proceeds}} = \text{installments}$$

fixed premium terms under which the amount of premium due remains level throughout the time the policy is in force, regardless of loss experience by the company. See also *estimated premium; experience modification.*

flat commission arrangement under which an agent is paid a predetermined scale of commissions, regardless of the type of policies sold. See also *agent; commission.*

flat schedule a form of group contract providing equal benefits for every member of the group, regardless of different levels of compensation, risk or need. See also *group contract.*

flexible premium annuity   a form of annuity allowing the annuitant to vary the premium payments, by amount, timing, or both. The contract establishes minimum levels required, with benefits varying based on the amount of premiums paid and the timing of those payments. See also *annuity; fixed premium.*

flexible premium life   a form of life insurance, also called variable premium life, in which the insured can vary the amount and timing of premium payments—within specified minimum levels. The change in premium payments will also change the amount of insurance in force. See also *fixed premium; life insurance; variable premium life.*

flexible premium variable life   universal life insurance including a fixed initial premium, after which the insured can vary the timing and amount of premium payments (within specified limits). The death benefit will vary according to the timing and amount of premiums, and also on the investment return from securities. See also *life insurance; universal variable life; variable life.* See illustration, page 77.

floater   an addition to an existing property and casualty insurance policy, often for personal property in addition to specified coverage already provided. See also *personal property; property and casualty insurance.*

foreign company   an insurance company not licensed to conduct business in a state. See also *domestic company; insurer; non-admitted company.*

forfeiture   **(1)** the loss of rights provided under the terms of a policy of insurance, due to lapse of the policy or violation of a contractual provision. **(2)** the loss of value or benefits in a pension plan due to termination of employment prior to full vesting. See also *nonforfeiture provision; pension plan; vesting.*

form   an application, endorsement, policy, rider or other document that is considered as part of the insurance contract. See also *application; endorsement; policy; rider.*

fortuitous loss   an unknown or unanticipated event that leads to a loss. Insurance policies provide protection against fortuitous losses. For example, although death is a certainty, the timing of death cannot be known. Life insurance provides protection against the economic loss resulting from the unexpected death of a wage earner. See also *loss.*

flexible premium variable life

PREMIUM

minimum required

DEATH BENEFIT

minimum guaranteed

---

fractional premium   a premium paid in a mode other than for one full year. Fractional premiums can be paid in monthly, quarterly or semiannual modes. See also *modal premium; premium.*

fraudulent misrepresentation   a statement or claim that is made falsely, to misrepresent the facts or mislead someone else. A claim for insurance will be contested if a false or misleading motive is proven, or if fraud is shown by statements made in the application. See also *contestability; incontestability.*

free examination   the right of a newly insured person to review the terms and conditions of an insurance policy for 10 days, without obligation. If, during that time, the insured decides not to continue the coverage, the initial premium must be returned, and the policy is cancelled. See also *initial premium.*

Free of Particular Average (FPA) a provision in marine insurance policies that is similar to the deductible provisions or coinsurance clauses in other types of policies. Losses will be paid in excess of a specified amount or percentage of the total asset's value. See also *coinsurance; deductible; marine insurance.*

front-end load descriptive of policies in which the expenses of selling insurance are calculated from the start of premium payments. See also *back-end load; load; no-load.*

full age the age of majority, after which an individual is legally able to enter contracts. This age is 18 or 21 in most states. See also *contract.*

full vesting attainment of all privileges and 100% of benefits in a retirement plan. Vesting may occur over a period of time, or granted from the moment of qualification, depending on the terms of a plan. See also *retirement plan; vesting.*

fully paid descriptive of a policy in which all premium payments have been made. The policy remains in force after the paid-up date, or can be converted to its cash value. See also *life insurance; paid-up insurance.*

fund money held in trust or in a pension plan, for use in later years. To build a fund when the amount of its future value is known, periodic payments are made each month or each year, with an assumed interest rate determining the amount of payment. See also *pension plan; trust.*

funded a pension plan that has received contributions and earned a collective sum of money adequate to pay all of its current and future obligations. See also *pension plan.*

G

GAAP requirements rules for reporting profits and losses, reserve levels, and placing value on an insurance company's assets. GAAP is an acronym for Generally Accepted Accounting Principles. Insurers report tax liabilities and complete their annual state financial reports on the statutory basis. However, that basis does not accurately report income and expenses during the same period. For example, an agent sells policies during the year and is paid first year commissions of 120% of total premiums received. On a statutory basis, all paid-out commissions are reported as current-year expenses. On a GAAP basis, the commission expense is deferred over the average expected in-force period of each policy. The same restatements apply to establishment of GAAP, versus statutory reserve levels. See also *Generally Accepted Accounting Principles (GAAP); statutory requirements.*

General Adjustment Bureau (GAB) an agency that provides member property and casualty insurance companies with claims adjustment services. See also *claim; property and casualty insurance.*

general agency an independent that represents life and health insurers through an independent office or string of offices. An agreement is entered into between the independent agency and the insurance company, specifying levels of compensation, competitive limits and provisions, and the actions of agents in the independent office. See also *agency; health insurance; independent agent; life insurance.*

General Agent (GA) an individual licensed to sell insurance, usually in the life and health categories, who works through a general agency. See also *agent; health insurance; independent agent; life insurance.*

General Agents and Managers Conference (GAMC) an affiliated agency of the National Association of Life Underwriters (NALU), whose purpose is to recognize performance of its own members, and to provide solutions to management problems in the life insurance industry. See also *life insurance; National Association of Life Underwriters (NALU); underwriting.*

general liability liability arising from omissions or negligence, injuries resulting from business operation, or product defects. See also *liability; negligence.*

Generally Accepted Accounting Principles (GAAP) the guidelines and rules established by the Financial Accounting Standards Board (FASB) for the accurate and consistent reporting of profits and losses, and for placing value on assets and liabilities. For insurance purposes, GAAP reporting differs substantially from statutory form (required by state law). GAAP reporting requires reporting of income and directly related costs and expenses over the identical period; stating of reserves on the basis of realistic expectation; valuing of investment assets on a sound market value basis; and other adjustments to the values and profits reported to the various states. See also *GAAP requirements; statutory accounting.*

government life insurance one of four forms of life insurance provided through the U.S. government to members of the armed forces. Programs include:

—Servicemen's Group Life Insurance (SGLI)—term insurance partially subsidized by the government and reinsured to private insurance companies.

—Veterans Group Life Insurance (VGLI)—a continuation of the SGLI program, allowing an insured member of the armed forces to convert a policy to 5-year term insurance.

—National Service Life Insurance (NSLU)—issued from 1940 to 1950, this provided between $1,000 and $10,000 of term or permanent life insurance.

—United States Government Life Insurance (USGLI)—a past program that provided members of the armed forces with up to $10,000 in renewable term life coverage.

See also *convertible term; life insurance; National Service Life Insurance (NSLI); reinsurance; Servicemen's Group Life Insurance (SGLI); United States Group Life Insurance (USGLI); Veterans Group Life Insurance (VGLI).*

grace period a 30-day period following a policy's premium due date, during which the premium can be paid without the threat of lapse. If, after the grace period, the premium is not paid, the insurer has a contractual right to cancel the policy. See also *lapse; premium.*

grace period

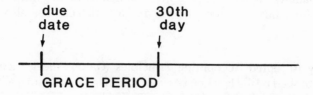

graded commission any form of compensation to an agent in which the level increases, based on volume, level of premium, or type of insurance sold. There are three forms of grading:

a) on the basis of the type of policy sold. An agent can be compensated at one level for selling one type of policy, with the provision that either a combination of two or more policies, or a specific type of policy will result in higher commissions.

b) by volume of total business. As an incentive, companies will promise to increase the level of commission when the agent's total volume exceeds a specified level within a given length of time.

c) for group policies. Some group commissions are paid at graded levels, depending on the total dollar amount of premium.
See also *commission; flat commission.*

graded death benefit   a provision in some forms of life insurance policies sold to young children, providing for the payment of a minimum amount at one age, and increasing benefits as the child grows. At a specified age, the full face value of the policy is payable in the event of death. See also *death benefit; face amount; life insurance.*

---

graded death benefit

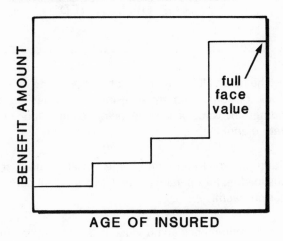

graded premium   a provision in certain modified life or whole life insurance policies, calling for increases in premium payments over time, until a specified level has been reached. Cash value builds more gradually in these policies, but the insured is better able to afford coverage during the early coverage years. See also *cash value; life insurance; modified life; premium; whole life insurance.*

---

graded premium

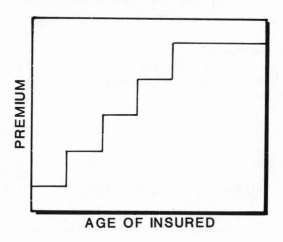

gross estate the total value of a decedent's estate at the time of death, including real and personal property, investments, savings, receivables, and business holdings; the value of an estate before computation of estate taxes. See also *estate planning.*

gross premium the total premium charged to an insured, including net premium plus loading for operating expenses and agent commissions. See also *load; net premium.*

group annuity a retirement plan provided by an employer, union, or other entity. The combination of employer and employee contributions is invested in a single group contract. Upon annuitization, each member of the group receives a proportionate share of benefits. See also *annuity; retirement plan.* See illustration, page 83.

group certificate a document given to each member of a group insurance plan. The certificate explains benefits under the policy, in summarized form.

group annuity

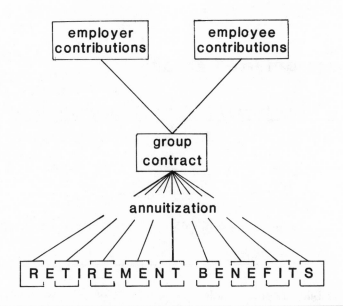

The master policy is retained by the employer or entity administering the contract in behalf of the group. See also *benefit; certificate of insurance; master policy; policy.*

group contract   a single insurance policy that spells out the terms and conditions. Life and health contracts specify the method of underwriting and qualifications or definitions of the group; benefits provided; and eligibility requirements. See also *eligibility requirements; health insurance; life insurance.*

group credit life   insurance provided on a group basis, protecting a lender in the event of the death of a borrower. When death occurs before full repayment of the debt, the lender is compensated by way of a benefit payment by the insurance company. See also *credit life; life insurance.*

group deferred annuity   a form of annuity in which employees or other members of a group contribute to a deferred annuity plan (or contributions are made in their behalf). Each contribution is used to buy paid-up annuities. Upon annuitization, each member is entitled to benefit payments. See also *allocated benefits; annuity; deferred annuity; single premium deferred annuity.*

---

group deferred annuity

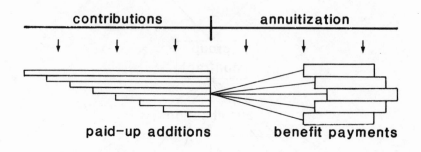

group disability income   a policy provided to employees, providing for the payment of benefits in the event of total or partial disability. Benefits are limited to a percentage of compensation (often 50% to 75%), and to the total period of time that benefits will be paid . See also *disability income; health insurance.*

group health   health insurance provided to a group of individuals sharing common characteristics. For example, the employees of one company, members of a union or club, or participants in a credit union may apply for group health insurance. The policy limits benefits through deductible and coinsurance clauses. For example, one policy begins paying benefits when health expenses exceed $200 per covered person during any one calendar year (deductible). From that level up, the insurer will pay 80% of covered services (coinsurance). See also *coinsurance; deductible; health insurance; true group plan.*

group life   life insurance provided to a group of people with common characteristics, such as the employees of one company. The plan often includes a related form of disability coverage, specifies the method of group underwriting, guarantees issue of coverage to all members of the group, and includes a conversion privilege to permanent insurance upon termination of employment. Death benefits are usually related to the level of compensation. For example, a policy might state that a death benefit equal to one year's salary will be paid, and allows employees to purchase additional insurance under the same plan up to 1.5 times annual salary. See also *conversion privilege; disability benefit; life insurance.*

guaranteed dividend   payments made to the insured as part of a coupon plan. Regular, guaranteed payments are made as part of the contractual agreement. This is a form of non-participating life insurance; a participating policy guarantees minimum dividend payment rates, but will also pay dividends above those levels, based on profits the company experiences during the year. The guaranteed dividend is actually a form of partial endowment, or reimbursement to the policyholder of part of the premiums previously paid. See also *coupon plan; dividend; life insurance; nonparticipating policy.*

guaranteed insurability   a privilege granted to an insured person in some forms of insurance policies. The individual has the right to buy additional insurance, or to convert one form of coverage to another, without having to submit to additional standards, such as a medical examination. The guarantee is granted at specified times, such as upon expiration of the 10th anniversary year; up until a maximum age as stated in the policy; or upon the occurrence of a stated event. For example, a policy provides that if the insured has a child, the level of insurance can be increased. See also *adverse selection; evidence of insurability; insurability; life insurance; rider.*

guaranteed rate of interest   a promise made by the insurance company, to pay a minimum level of interest to a permanent life insurance policyholder each year. See also *interest rate; permanent life; rate of return; reserve.*

guaranteed renewable   a form of health insurance allowing the insured to continue coverage upon the expiration of a stated term. The company cannot cancel the policy or modify provisions. However, the premium can be increased based on standards that are applied to everyone. Example: A company increases the premium rate based on the age of all insured persons with one form of policy. See also *cancellation provision; insurability; noncancellable guaranteed renewable.*

guardian   an individual responsible for managing and caring for a person who is not legally of age to act independently; or who is not mentally capable of caring for himself. See also *administrator.*

guardian of the person   a distinction of guardianship that is limited to care of a person who is legally or mentally unable. See also *administrator.*

guardian of the property a distinction of guardianship limited to the management and care of property belonging to a minor or a person who is mentally incapable. See also *administrator.*

guideline premium the minimum or average premium the insured is expected to pay each year in a universal life insurance policy, to provide insurance and endowment benefits required by the terms of the contract. See also *life insurance; premium; universal life.*

H

hazard insurance a provision in fire insurance policies excluding coverage for hazards known to the insured person. It is assumed that losses could be prevented, or that special dangers were known to the insured because the hazard existed, and that the insurance company was not informed of the danger. Example: A homeowner stores several cans of gasoline in his basement. A fire destroys the entire house. If the gasoline was not stored on the premises, the actual loss could have been less severe, but the homeowner knew of the hazard and did nothing to prevent it, such as removing the gasoline. See also *fire insurance; loss prevention.*

health insurance a range of insurance against the economic consequences of unexpected health problems, including hospitalization, disability, accidental death; and long-term hospital stays. See also *accident and health; disability income; major medical.*

Health Insurance Association of America (HIAA) a lobbying and educational association whose purpose is to educate the public about the necessity of private insurance coverage. See also *accident and health.*

Health Insurance Institute (HII) a public relations association supported by member life and health insurance companies, to provide the public with information about their products and services. See also *accident and health.*

Health Maintenance Organization (HMO) a form of health insurance combining a range of coverages in a group basis. The group approach reduces premium costs when compared to individual policies. Members are allowed to select their own physicians, and receive hospital, outpatient, and in-hospital physician services. Members are often required to pay a flat fee per visit, a co-payment assessed in addition to their premiums. See also *co-payment; group health.*

heir   an individual entitled to receive the assets of a deceased person, either by will or by relationship in the case of an intestate death. See also *beneficiary; estate planning; intestacy property.*

HO-1   homeowner's insurance providing coverage only to the extent of 11 named perils, also called the basic policy. See also *basic policy; casualty insurance; liability insurance.*

HO-2   homeowner's insurance providing coverage for 18 named perils, also called the broad form. See also *broad form; casualty insurance; liability insurance.*

HO-3   homeowner's insurance that provides protection against all losses except named exclusions on the insured's dwelling; and for 18 named perils for personal property. HO-3 is also known as the all risks form. See also *all risks; casualty insurance; liability insurance.*

HO-4   homeowner's insurance protecting against 18 named perils for personal property only; designed for those renting property. The owner is responsible for insurance on the building. HO-4 is also called the renter's policy. See also *casualty insurance; liability insurance; renter's policy.*

HO-5   the most complete form of homeowner's insurance, including protection against all risks except named exclusions, also known as the comprehensive policy. See also *casualty insurance; comprehensive policy; liability insurance.*

HO-6   homeowner's insurance providing all risks protection on personal property, but no coverage on losses to the building. This policy is designed for owners of condominiums or cooperative housing. The association is responsible for insuring the building and common areas. HO-6 is also called the condominium policy. See also *casualty insurance; condominium policy; liability insurance.*

HO-8   homeowner's insurance especially designed for older homes. It covers 11 named perils, and promises to restore lost property to serviceable condition—but not with the same quality of materials or workmanship. See also *casualty insurance; liability insurance; older homes policy.*

Home Office Life Underwriters Association (HOLUA) an association whose members are life insurance company underwriters working in the company's home office. The association provides education information and materials to its members, and also administers a qualifications exam. See also *life underwriter; underwriting.*

homeowner's insurance protection for owners or renters against losses resulting from fire, theft, vandalism, and other losses. The policy provides both liability and casualty protection.

Liability arises from losses to others in connection with property. For example, a visitor is injured on the premises and has medical expenses or files a claim for pain and suffering. Or a neighbor's property is damaged when a limb from a homeowner's tree falls into their roof. In these cases, claims would be paid under the liability section of the homeowner's policy.

Casualty protection includes losses due to fire, losses due to weather and natural causes, vandalism, theft, and other causes. Four types of casualty protection are included in the policy: the home itself, unattached structures (such as garages and storage sheds), personal property, and additional living expenses. Example: After a fire, a policyowner and his family move to a hotel until the damage can be repaired. The additional living expenses are reimbursed by the insurance company.

Homeowner's insurance can be purchased to match each owner's or renter's situation. Owners of condominiums and cooperatives do not need insurance on the building, as that is provided by the association. So their policies provide only personal property and liability coverage. Casualty insurance can be purchased to provide three levels of coverage:

1. Eleven named perils. Policies will reimburse only those losses caused by:
   —fire or lightning
   —loss of property removed from the premises because of fire and other perils
   —windstorm or hail
   —explosion
   —riots and civil commotion
   —aircraft
   —vehicles
   —smoke
   —vandalism and malicious mischief
   —theft
   —breakage of glass as part of the building
2. Eighteen named perils. These policies extend coverage to losses caused by the 11 named perils, plus damage from:
   —falling objects

—weight of ice or snow

—collapse of a building

—sudden tearing apart, cracking, burning or bulging of steam or hot water systems or appliances for heating water

—accidental discharge, leakage or overflow from a plumbing, heating, or air conditioning system or appliance

—freezing of plumbing, heating, and air conditioning systems and appliances

—sudden and accidental injury from electrical currents of appliances, fixtures and wiring

3. All risks. This form of insurance protects against all losses except those specifically excluded. Common exclusions are flood, earthquake, acts of war and nuclear accident.

Casualty protection can be purchased on the basis of Actual Cash Value (ACV), a form of reimbursement based on cost, minus depreciation. For example, you bought a television set 10 years ago for $700. The insurance company determines that $40 per year should be deducted for depreciation, for a total of $400. Only $300—current depreciated value—will be paid following a loss.

An alternative is to purchase the more expensive replacement cost insurance. This will replace lost items not on a depreciated basis, but at a level required to repurchase at today's price. However, replacement cost is limited. For example, a policy might specify that replacement cost cannot exceed 400% of computed ACV. A homeowner bought furniture 15 years ago for $3,700. After depreciation under the ACV computation, that furniture is worth only $600 today. With the 400% limitation, replacement cost coverage would pay only $2,400 ($600 × 400%).

Casualty protection can also be purchased with periodic increases in coverage limits for inflation. In the event that a home's value increases, or the value of personal possessions grows due to inflation, the so-called inflation guard adds extra insurance. The provision is tied to an independent index, such as the Consumer Price Index. However, this provision does not protect homeowners who fail to review and upgrade their coverage at least once per year. Every homeowner or renter should take these steps to ensure adequate protection:

1. Review policy coverages no less than annually, and modify the type and scope of insurance as needed.

2. Take physical or videotaped inventory of all possessions, and keep the inventory off the premises.

3. Consult with a professional insurance agent to determine the best form of coverage.

4. To estimate the level of coverage required for personal possessions, assume value to equal the value of the home itself. (In the past, agents

recommended 50% of a home's value for personal possessions. Recent trends, however, show that homeowners tend to match their homes' value with personal possessions of approximately the same value). For example, if property is valued at $100,000, it should be assumed that an additional $100,000 of insurance is needed for personal property.

Policies limit coverage for cash on the premises, rare collections, art, jewelry, furs, and other items. Riders or separate insurance is needed for these. Also excluded from the standard policy are assets for a business in the home, as well as liabilities arising from conduct of business. Riders should be purchased to extend coverage to professional activities. See also *Actual Cash Value (ACV); all risks; basic policy; broad form; casualty insurance; comprehensive policy; condominium policy; depreciation; liability insurance; older homes policy; renter's policy; replacement cost.* See illustration, page 91.

hospital indemnity   extension of a health insurance policy to include the cost of a hospital stay and related expenses. See also *health insurance; indemnity.*

hospitalization insurance   protection against the cost of daily room charges and other hospitalization costs, often as part of major medical coverage in addition to accident and health insurance. See also *accident and health; health insurance; major medical.*

I

identification   a phase in the process of risk management, involving the definition of losses. A source, or the combined source of contingent losses or actual past losses, is traced and methods are then derived to minimize future risks or to remove contributing causes. See also *risk management.*

immediate annuity   a form of annuity in which periodic benefits begin at the end of the first month or quarter, following payment of a single premium. See also *annuity; deferred annuity.* See illustration, page 92.

immediate vesting   the right of an employee to receive full benefits of a retirement plan, from the moment that participation begins. In comparison, a deferred vesting program requires the employee to meet qualifications of time, and vests gradually or all at once, after that time has passed. See also *deferred vesting; retirement plan; vesting.*

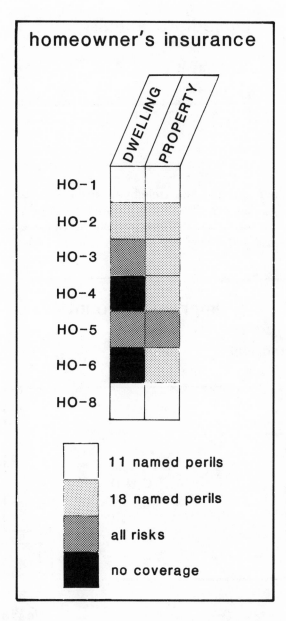

homeowner's insurance

DWELLING | PROPERTY

HO-1
HO-2
HO-3
HO-4
HO-5
HO-6
HO-8

11 named perils

18 named perils

all risks

no coverage

impaired risk   also known as a substandard risk, descriptive of an individual who cannot qualify for standard rates of insurance. The decision is based on age, health conditions, occupation, dangerous hobbies, or a combination of these factors. See also *health insurance; life insurance; risk; substandard risk.*

immediate annuity

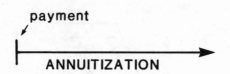

imprest account   any fund that is reimbursed to the extent of expenses paid out. As part of a plan for self-insurance, the fund is established at a specified level. As claims are paid an equal amount is put back into the fund, restoring it to the pre-established level. See also *loss; self-insurance.*

imprest account

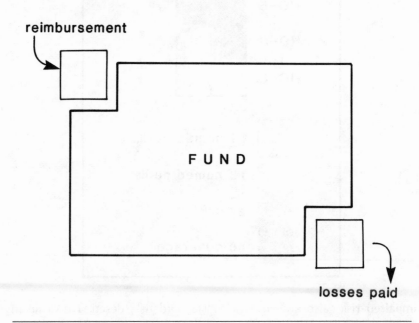

in force   (1) in life insurance, the total face amount of insurance for which the company is at risk. For example, every $100,000 policy sold adds that amount to the total in force. When claims are paid, or when insurance policies lapse or terminate, the in force total is reduced. **(2)** in health insurance, the total volume of premium being collected on active policies carried by the insurer. See also *face amount; health insurance; life insurance; premium.*

income participation   the sharing of divisible surplus among the owners of participating policies. A dividend is declared and credited to the policy-owner, under one of several settlement options. For example, one policy-owner receives dividends in cash; another leaves dividends on deposit to accumulate at interest; a third applies dividends to the purchase of additional paid-up insurance; and a fourth applies dividends to reduce premiums. See also *dividend; divisible surplus; life insurance; participating policy.*

income replacement   the formula applied to the purchase of disability income insurance. The amount of insurance is tied to the monthly income the insured earns. Because disability benefits are free of income taxes, it is not necessary to replace 100% of gross earnings. In most policies, the disability benefit is computed as a percentage of monthly earnings. See also *benefit; disability income.*

incontestability   a clause in life insurance policies specifying that the company cannot cancel the policy or change its premium and other terms, after the expiration of a contestability period. This is usually two years. After that time, the only basis for contesting a claim is proof of fraud. Example: A policyowner knows he has a terminal disease at the time he purchases an insurance policy. He dies after three years from the policy date. The insurer cannot contest the claim in the belief of prior knowledge, unless it can prove fraud. However, with the insured already deceased, it would be very difficult to prove intent. See also *contestability; life insurance.*

increased hazard   a condition that exceeds the risk limitations the insurance company intended to cover at the time a policy was issued. This may serve as the basis for denying or reducing a claim. Example: A policyowner buys a health insurance policy, and states on the application that he does not pursue any dangerous hobbies. Later, he begins skydiving as a recreational pursuit. The insurer could suspend or modify the policy because of the increased hazard. See also *hazard insurance; health insurance; property and casualty insurance; risk.*

Incurred But Not Reported (IBNR)   a term describing losses that an insurer has not learned about at the end of a period of time. Example: At the end of the reporting year, the insurer closes its books. The insurer knows that among its thousands of policies, some claims have probably occurred and have not yet been submitted. A reserve is established for these losses, based on historic averages. See also *loss; reserve.*

incurred loss   any loss for which the insurer is liable for payment of a claim, whether that claim has been paid or not. The distinction between "incurred" and "paid" is an important one. At the beginning and end of a year, a varying level of claims might be incurred and paid. Some claim payments refer to losses incurred in a past period, while some incurred losses are not paid until a future period. For accuracy in year-to-year comparisons, incurred loss trends are tracked. See also *loss.*

Incurred Loss Ratio (ILR)   a ratio comparing incurred losses to earned premiums. This shows the percentage of premium income that goes to the payment of losses each month, quarter or year. For example, a company has incurred losses one year for a particular line of business totaling $12,418,000. During that same period, it earns $14,192,000 in premium. Its ILR is 87.5%. See also *earned premium; loss.*

Incurred Loss Ratio (ILR)

$$\frac{\text{incurred losses}}{\text{earned premium}}$$

$$\frac{\$12,418,000}{\$14,192,000} = 87.5\%$$

indemnity (1) payment of a claim in a property and casualty policy. Indemnification is intended to restore the insured to the condition prior to the loss. Example: A homeowner has insurance adequate to replace a home in the event of a casualty. A fire destroys the house and all belongings. Indemnity in this instance will return the value of the home and personal property. **(2)** in life insurance, the amount of payment a beneficiary receives. It might be far greater than the expected benefit, or the amount of premiums paid to date. Example: An individual earns $45,000 per year, and purchases a life insurance policy that will pay $250,000 in the event of death. A week after making the first payment, the individual passes away. The beneficiary will receive the full $250,000. In this case, the potential earnings over a lifetime are partly or fully indemnified; or the immediate loss is compensated for by payment of the face amount. See also *benefit; life insurance; loss; property and casualty insurance.*

independent agent   an insurance agent who represents two or more insurance companies for customers' needs. The independent agent is able to compare rates, and to offer a wider range of insurance products to customers, than a captive agent. See also *agent; captive agent; direct writer; General Agent (GA).*

independent agent

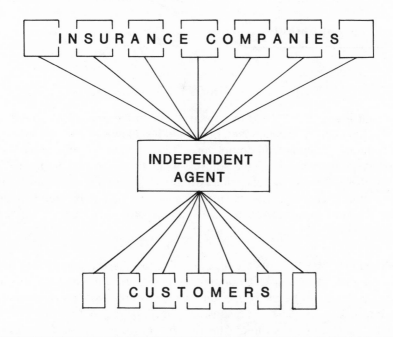

Independent Insurance Agents of America (IIAA)   a professional association that lobbies and provides education to its agent members. See also *agent.*

indeterminate premium life   also known as adjustable life, a form of non-participating life insurance in which a relatively low initial premium is paid for a specified period of time; it then increases on a predetermined formula. During both periods, the maximum amount the insurer is allowed to charge is fixed by formula. The maximum premium is guaranteed, based on the insurer's expected mortality. See also *adjustable life; expected mortality; life insurance; non-participating policy.*

indeterminate premium life

maximum

maximum   **ADJUSTMENT**   future period

initial period

indexed life   a form of life insurance in which the amount of premiums varies based on an independent, outside index. However, the face amount and ultimate death benefit do not vary. This method of paying on a life insurance policy is similar to the adjustable rate mortgage used in many real estate loans. The contract of insurance may specify a periodic maximum that the premium can be increased, and may also specify a maximum increase over the term of insurance. See also *contract; death benefit; face amount; life insurance.*

indirect loss   any form of casualty or liability loss that is not directly caused by an event. For example, a homeowner is distraught following a fire that destroys the family home. As a result, he is away from work for an extended period of time. The loss of possessions and property is a direct loss, while the loss of earnings is indirect. See also *direct loss; loss; property and casualty insurance.*

individual account plan   a form of pension plan or profit sharing plan in which the employer, trustee or administrator establishes one account for each participant. In comparison, a more common method is to treat all contributions as a pool, and to pay out benefits on a prescribed sharing formula. See also *pension plan; profit sharing plan.*

---

individual account plan

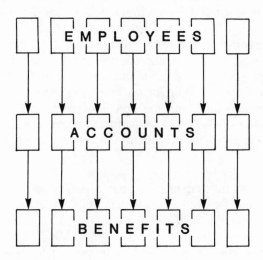

---

individual insurance   forms of insurance protection written for one person per policy, as opposed to the insuring of a group having similar characteristics. See also *group contract.*

Individual Level Cost Method (ILCM)   a method of estimating payments that must be made over a period of time in a defined benefit plan. A known future amount must be established, and an assumed rate of earnings on accumulation is used. The purpose is to determine the level of periodic payments between the date of qualification and the targeted retirement age. See also *defined benefit plan; pension plan; retirement age.*

Individual Retirement Account (IRA)   a retirement account for individuals. Up to $2,000 per year is deposited with a trustee or custodian. All earnings are tax deferred until funds are withdrawn. Depending on levels of other, taxable income, all or part of the IRA contribution may be deducted from gross income, thus reducing current year taxes. If the individual also participates in a separate retirement account, the IRA contribution is not deductible. This rule took effect starting in 1987, as a provision of the Tax Reform Act of 1986. Prior to that date, every individual was allowed to deduct IRA contributions, whether or not they participated in separate plans. Withdrawal is scheduled to begin at any time after age 59½. If funds are withdrawn prior to that date, and provided tax deferral benefits in the year claimed, all withdrawals are taxable. In addition, withdrawals are subject to tax penalties. Rules for deduction of IRA contributions on a state level vary by state. See also *qualified plan; retirement plan; tax deferral.*

Individual Retirement Annuity (IRA)   an annuity that is scheduled to begin benefits following a targeted retirement age, as all or part of an individual retirement plan. Payments of premiums might or might not be applied to reduce annual gross income for tax purposes, depending on the status of the plan and on other income and retirement plans the individual has. The annuity can also be an Individual Retirement Account in which the annuity is the principal investment. See also *annuity; retirement plan; tax deferral.*

industrial life   also called debit insurance, a form of life insurance, usually issued in very small face values, on which premiums are paid weekly. See also *debit insurance; life insurance.*

inflation endorsement   a provision in a property and casualty insurance policy that increases the maximum coverage for inflation. The graded benefit is tied to an independent index, such as the Consumer Price Index. See also *endorsement; property and casualty insurance; replacement cost.*

inheritance   value passed from the deceased person to his or her heirs. See also *estate planning; heir; legacy.*

inheritance tax   a tax on the value of an inheritance, charged at the state level. The tax is levied against the estate, and not the individual who inherits it. See also *estate tax.*

initial premium   the first modal premium (monthly, quarterly, semiannual, or annual) paid at the inception of the policy. Payment of the premium usually constitutes the beginning of the contract of insurance. See also *contract of insurance; modal premium; premium.*

initial reserve   the reserve established at the beginning of the policy year, consisting of the previous year's ending terminal reserve, plus the annual net premium. See also *annual premium; life insurance; reserve; terminal reserve.*

inland marine   a specialized form of property and casualty insurance, including coverage against losses occurring during shipment of goods. Coverage extends to fire, theft, weather damage, derailment, and collision, for example. A number of specialized inland marine coverages can be purchased separately or as additional provisions. See also *liability insurance; property and casualty insurance.*

Inland Marine Underwriters Association (IMUA)   an association whose members include professionals in the inland marine insurance business. See also *underwriting.*

inspection   (1) a contractual provision in property and casualty insurance policies, allowing the company to visit a site and check for risks or special dangers, either before issuing the policy or as a condition for renewal. (2) an audit of the payroll records by the carrier of a workers compensation insurance policy. (3) an examination of damaged property, conducted by a claims adjuster to evaluate and put a value on the loss. (4) a review of an application for insurance, and related outside reviews such as medical and credit history, conducted as part of the underwriting process. See also *application; liability insurance; loss prevention; property and casualty insurance; underwriting; workers compensation.*

inspection report   a report issued by an independent inspection bureau, following submission of an application for insurance. The report includes medical, financial, lifestyle, and other types of information. See also *risk selection; underwriting.*

installment deferred annuity   any annuity in which a series of premium payments are made over time. At annuitization—a date identified by the number of years premiums have been paid, or the annuitant's age—the premium payments stop and the insurance company begins making periodic benefit payments. See also *annuity; deferred annuity; single premium deferred annuity.* See illustration, page 100.

installment refund annuity   an annuity that includes a provision promising to repay no less than a guaranteed amount. Either the annuitant or a beneficiary will receive this amount, even if the annuitant passes away before the refund period expires. In the event that the annuitant outlives the refund period, payments will continue for life. See also *annuity; certain payment; refund annuity.* See illustration, page 100.

installment deferred annuity

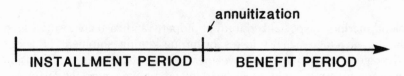

annuitization

|—————————————————————————|———————————————————————————————►
    INSTALLMENT PERIOD   BENEFIT PERIOD

installment refund annuity

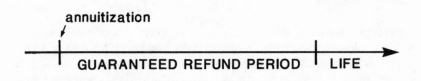

annuitization

————|—————————————————————————|———————————————————►
        GUARANTEED REFUND PERIOD   LIFE

Institute of Life Insurance (ILI)   an association supported by member life insurance companies, intended to promote a positive image of the industry. See also *life insurance.*

insurability   qualification for insurance, by the standards of the insurance company. In risk evaluation, current health and health history, age of the applicant, occupation and exposure to perils, hobbies, lifestyle, all combine to make the individual an acceptable or an unacceptable risk. When some factors are present, the individual might be insurable as a substandard risk, meaning premium payments will be higher, or that certain types of perils might be excluded from coverage. Example: an applicant for health insurance has a history of chronic kidney problems. The insurance company offers to underwrite the risk with an exclusion for all kidney-related illnesses. See also *rated policy; risk; standard risk; substandard risk; uninsurable risk.*

insurable interest   the interest an individual must have in insurance coverage carried by someone else. This is an important test in determining the motive for purchasing insurance, and in the assignment of a beneficiary in a life insurance policy. Example: A wage earner applies for life insurance, and names a spouse and children as beneficiaries. The insurance company recognizes that, in the event of the unexpected death of the insured person, the family would suffer an economic loss. Accordingly, they have an insurable interest. Example: One individual offers to pay the premiums on a life insurance policy of another person, if that person will name him as beneficiary. The insurance company will not issue the policy on this basis, as it is a wager rather than a contract for insurance. See also *beneficiary; wagering.*

insurable risk   a risk that qualifies for insurance coverage. A "risk" might be property, or the health or life of an individual or group. See also *fortuitous loss; risk; uninsurable risk.*

Insurance Accounting and Statistical Association (IASA)   an association whose members work in actuarial, accounting and statistical occupations within the life insurance industry. See also *life insurance.*

insurance contract   a unilateral contract between the insurance company and the insured. The company promises to pay the insured if and when specified losses occur. Terms—premium, term, coinsurance, length of coverage, and exclusions—are spelled out in the contract. In return, the insured agrees to pay premiums. See also *contract; unilateral contract.*

Insurance Economic Society of America (IESA)   a public relations society whose purpose is to educate the public about the workings of the insurance industry. See also *individual insurance.*

Insurance Information Institute (III)   a public relations association for member property and casualty insurance companies, whose purpose is to promote a positive image of the industry. See also *property and casualty insurance.*

Insurance Institute of America (IIA)   an association of insurance professionals, which organizes and administers examinations for supervisors and managers, in topics such as risk management and underwriting. See also *risk management; underwriting.*

Insurance Regulatory Information System (IRIS)   a set of standards for financial analysis in life, health and property and casualty insurance companies, organized and published by the National Association of Insurance Commissioners (NAIC). IRIS includes yield and ratio analysis of admitted assets, investments, expenses, capital surplus, written premium, and losses. See also *investment net income; National Association of Insurance Commissioners (NAIC); written premium.*

Insurance Service Association of America (ISAA)   an association whose membership includes insurance agents. See also *agent.*

Insurance Services Office (ISO)   an organization that assists property and casualty insurance companies in the development of rates, based on loss experience of the industry as a whole. This service is especially useful to smaller companies that cannot afford to develop their own internal actuarial systems. See also *experience; property and casualty insurance.*

insured   the individual who holds a policy of insurance. The policyholder is distinguished from the policyowner, who might not be the same person. See also *policyholder.*

insurer   the company that issues a policy in exchange for a stated commission, and assumes the risk of loss. See also *policy; risk.*

insuring agreement   a section of the contract of insurance that details the extent of coverage being provided. It specifies the limits of that coverage, while named exclusions are listed in another section. See also *contract of insurance; policy.*

intangible property   property without physical form, including covenants, rights, options, and easements. See also *personal property; property and casualty insurance.*

integration   the coordinated benefits that will be provided by a disability or retirement plan, based on total needs, less the Social Security benefits that the insured or employee will receive. See also *disability income; income replacement.*

interest   (1) earnings on invested money other than from capital gains or dividends; the compounded payment for the use of money. (2) the rights an individual has based on contingent economic effects of losses on the life or property of another. For example, an insurable interest is held by someone who is economically dependent upon someone else. See also *insurable interest; investment income.*

Interest Adjusted Cost (IAC)   a method for comparing the cost of different life insurance policies, based on the assumed amount of money needed in the event of death. IAC helps make comparisons valid, where other methods might not consider varying terms of policies. IAC assumes a rate of interest on money, and allows for the number of years until policy maturity. See also *accumulated value; actuarial present value; life insurance; time value of money.*

interest assumption   the estimated rate of return expected to be earned, used for the purpose of calculating future value or the amount needed in insurance reserves. An insurance company assumes it will earn a rate of interest, and bases its reserve requirements and amount of premium on that assumption. See also *life insurance; premium; rate of return; reserve.*

interest only option   one of several optional settlement modes for participating life insurance policies. When this option is selected, interest is not paid out to the policyholder, but left with the company to accumulate at compound interest. In some instances, dividends are paid out, used to reduce future premiums, or applied to the purchase of additional paid-up insurance. At the same time, an accumulated fund of interest only is left with the company to accumulate at interest. See also *guaranteed rate of interest; life insurance; optional settlement mode; participating policy; settlement option.*

interest rate   a percentage paid by a borrower to the lender or investor, for the use of money. A nominal, or stated rate will vary depending on method of compounding. See also *compound interest; investment income.*

interest sensitive insurance   a form of whole life insurance in which premiums are fixed, but cash value varies depending on interest earned. The insurance company places premiums in various investments. If they are profitable, the cash value increases; if not, it decreases. Such policies state minimum guarantees of cash value for the policyowner. See also *fixed premium; life insurance; whole life insurance.*

International Association of Health Underwriters (IAHU)   an association whose members work in the selling and underwriting of health insurance. See also *health insurance; underwriting.*

International Claim Association (ICA)   an association for professionals in the claim settlement business. See also *claim; settlement.*

inter-vivos trust   a form of trust that exists while its grantor is alive. In comparison, a testamentary trust takes effect upon the death of the grantor. See also *estate planning; living trust; testamentary trust; trust.*

intestacy property   property that was owned by a deceased person, when that person did not specify by will who should inherit it. Distribution is made through the laws of intestacy. See also *heir; laws of intestacy; testator; will.*

intestate descriptive of an individual who, at the time of death, does not have a valid will. See also *estate planning; testator; will.*

investment income income from interest, dividends, rental income and capital gains. Insurance companies invest in bonds, common and preferred stocks, mortgages and real estate. However, the company is required in reporting its net worth to exclude a portion of these investments. The purpose is to state the value of invested assets on a conservative level. In addition, specified limits of admitted assets can be invested in each category. See also *admitted assets; portfolio.*

investment net income the net amount earned by the insurance company, after deducting the cost of making investments and any losses experienced. For federal income tax purposes, insurers are taxed on either net income from insurance operations or from investment net income; but not on both. See also *net interest earned; rate of return.*

irrevocable beneficiary a beneficiary that cannot be removed from a policy without the beneficiary's written permission. See also *beneficiary; revocable beneficiary.*

irrevocable trust a trust that cannot be revoked by the grantor. See also *estate planning; revocable trust; trust.*

issue the children and other heirs of parents, including children, adopted children, grandchildren, and other direct descendants. See also *beneficiary; heir; life insurance; will.*

J

joint and survivors clause a provision in a life insurance policy issued on two lives, specifying that a death benefit will be paid only upon the death of the latest surviving spouse. See also *last survivors life; life insurance.*

joint life and survivors annuity a form of life annuity that guarantees to continue benefit payments for a certain period, and for as long as either spouse is living. The annuity contract often calls for a reduced payment following the death of the first person covered under the plan. See also *annuity certain; life annuity certain; survivorship annuity.*

---

joint life and survivors annuity

benefit period

| LIFE |
| LIFE |

---

joint and survivors insurance   a form of life insurance in which two lives, often a married couple, are insured under one policy. The death benefit is to be paid only upon the death of the last surviving spouse. See also *death benefit; life insurance.*

---

joint and survivors insurance

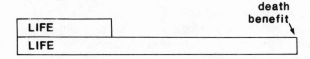

death benefit

| LIFE |
| LIFE |

Joint Tenancy with Rights of Survivorship (JTWROS)   a form of ownership registration over property, in which two or more common owners hold equal and undivided interests. In the event of the death of one owner, the surviving person(s) automatically receives proportionate ownership. Ownership is not transferred by will or under provisions of state laws of intestacy for property held under JTWROS registration. See also *laws of intestacy; tenants in common.*

joint tenants   individuals who own property or rights together. In the event of death, the surviving tenant automatically receives full ownership rights. See also *tenants in common.*

K

Keogh plan   a qualified plan designed for individuals who are self-employed. The plan was developed as part of the 1962 Self-Employed Individuals Tax Retirement Act, a bill also known as HR-10. Prior to the Keogh legislation, self-employed people could not enjoy the tax-deferral benefits that corporate employees had under pension and retirement plans.

A self-employed individual with no other sources of income can benefit by establishing a Keogh plan. Other than minimal benefits of Social Security, this is the only opportunity to accumulate retirement funds.

Provisions and benefits of the Keogh plan are similar to those of the IRA, but with different annual maximums. Contributions are made each year up to 25% of net earned income from self-employment activities. The 25% limitation assumes the contribution is already computed; as a result, the actual contribution is 20% of net income. (Example: Net earnings are $10,000. The self-employed individual may contribute as much as $2,000 to a Keogh plan. This represents 20% of the net, or 25% of the net *after* deducting the contribution itself.)

The amount contributed each year is deducted from gross income, and is thus tax-deferred until withdrawal. In addition, all income in the Keogh account is also tax-deferred. Withdrawals may begin at any time after the individual reaches age 59½. If funds are withdrawn before that date, they are subject to a penalty and immediate taxation. Early withdrawal can be taken without penalty only in the event of total disability, or by beneficiaries in the event of the self-employed person's death.

The maximum annual contribution to a Keogh plan is $30,000. However, the individual is not required to contribute the maximum in any one year. The Keogh account must be established with a trustee no later than December 31 of the applicable beginning tax year, and must be funded by the later of April 15 or the extended due date of that year's federal income tax return. See also *financial plan; Individual Retirement Account (IRA); qualified plan; retirement plan; tax deferral.*

key employee insurance   also called key-man or key executive insurance, a form of life, health or disability coverage on a partner, stockholder or employee. The company is the beneficiary, and will receive benefits—or is indemnified against losses—in the event of poor health, accidents or death. This form of insurance protects other owners against the losses that would result if the company would be liable for medical or support payments; or if the loss would result in a controlling interest transferring to outside owners.

Example: A partnership purchases key employee life insurance on each partner, with the partnership named as beneficiary. In the event of death, proceeds are to be used to purchase the deceased partner's equity share. See also *health insurance; life insurance.*

L

lapse   the cancellation of insurance due to the insured's failure to make premium payments. A life insurance policy that has built up cash value has a surrender value upon lapse, in which case a lapse is referred to as termination. See also *health insurance; life insurance; property and casualty insurance; surrender value; termination.*

Lapse Ratio (LR)   a calculation of the trend in lapsed policies from one year to the next. It involves dividing the policies lapsed in one year, by the number of policies in force at the beginning of that year. An increasing percentage is a negative trend for the company. Beginning-year in force statistics are used to exclude lapses of policies written during the year, as that would destroy the year-to-year trend. Policies are most likely to lapse in the first one to two months in force. For example, 13,407 policies lapsed during the year. At the beginning of that year, there were 94,584 policies of that type in force. The Lapse Ratio is 14.2%. See also *in force; surrender value; termination rate.* See illustration, page 108.

last survivor annuity   an annuity that continues payments as long as either of two spouses is alive. See also *joint and survivors insurance; survivorship annuity.*

last survivor life   a form of life insurance that will pay a death benefit only when the second spouse deceases. See also *joint life and survivors insurance.*

law of large numbers   a mathematical theory that probability is more accurate when a large sample is studied. The larger the base, the more accurate the average, and the lower the rate of deviation. The law of large

Lapse Ratio (LR)

lapsed policies
───────────────────────────
in force, beginning of the year

$$\frac{13,407}{94,584} = 14.2\%$$

numbers applies to morbidity in health insurance and to mortality in life insurance. The establishment of premium levels and reserves is based on
statistical probabilities of the number of losses per year. This is based on age,
risk exposure, and geographic factors. See also *exposure to loss; morbidity;
mortality; probability.*

law of large numbers

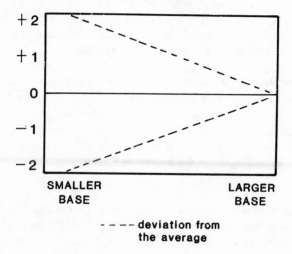

SMALLER   LARGER
BASE   BASE

- - - - deviation from
the average

laws of intestacy   state laws specifying how property is to be distributed in the event a deceased person has not drawn a will. See also *estate planning; intestacy property; will.*

layering   the process of covering all or part of a contingent loss with several policies. For example, the insured person or company wants to insure against as much as $500,000 of loss. The first insurance company will cover only $100,000; the second and third insurers each insure to a maximum of $200,000. This risk-spreading technique is the same as if one company insured the full $500,000, and then ceded part of its total risk to other insurers. See also *coinsurance; reinsurance; retention; risk.*

layering

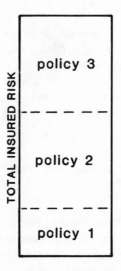

lead insurer   a company that underwrites a risk and then pools part of that risk. For example, a company writes a policy for $500,000, and then cedes $100,000 to three other companies. See also *reinsurance; retention; risk.* See illustration, page 110.

Leading Producers Round Table (LPRT)   an award granted to agents in the health insurance field by the International Association of Health

lead insurer

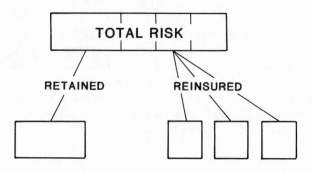

Underwriters (IAHU), in recognition of high sales volume. See also *health insurance; International Association of Health Underwriters (IAHU).*

leasehold insurance   a form of casualty insurance written to the lessor. In the event of a fire or other casualty, the insurance company will reimburse lost income that otherwise would have been earned under the conditions of the lease. Benefits will continue for as long as the premises cannot be leased, or if the lease is cancelled, as compensation for the direct loss of continuing income until the premises are again leased out. See also *casualty insurance; fire insurance.*

legacy   a bequest; the gift of property to other persons upon the death of an individual, as specified in a will. See also *estate planning; will.*

legal purpose   a point in contract law, that the contract must be in compliance with public policy and the law. Failing this, the contract is void. A life insurance contract, for example, must be entered into for the purpose of protecting against the economic consequences of an unexpected death. An individual who pays premiums on the life of another, but who has no insurable interest in that person, does not meet the legal purpose requirements of the contract. It is then not insurance, but a wager. See also *contract; insurable interest; void contract; wagering.*

legal reserve   the liability an insurance company establishes in compliance with state regulations, for each type of policy. The reserve must be estimated as the adequate present value of all future claims. See also *life insurance; present value; reserve; statutory reserves.*

legal reserve company a life insurance company that establishes its reserve according to the laws of those states in which it conducts business. See also *insurer; life insurance; reserve.*

letters testamentary written authorization from the court in a probate estate, instructing the executor to act according to the terms of a will. See also *probate estate; will.*

level commission a form of compensating insurance agents, in which the amount of commission is identical each year a policy is in force. In practice, level commissions are rare. Agents are more often compensated by way of an unusually high first year commission, followed by minimal renewal payments. See also *agent; commission; first year commission; flat commission.*

level commission

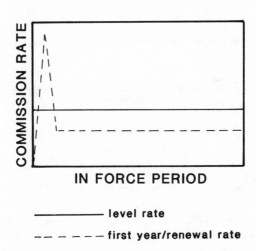

IN FORCE PERIOD

———————— **level rate**

— — — — — — **first year/renewal rate**

level premium descriptive of any policy with the provision that premiums will not change for the entire duration of the policy. This is common in whole life insurance policies. Term policies grant level premiums for the term, and may guarantee renewal without evidence of insurability. However, upon renewal, premium levels are adjusted in consideration of the insured's age. See also *fixed premium; premium.*

level term a form of term insurance in which the amount of coverage remains the same. In comparison, decreasing term's face value declines over the term. A level term period may be renewed for subsequent terms, in which case, premium levels are increased with each renewal. See also *decreasing term life; face amount; term life.*

level term

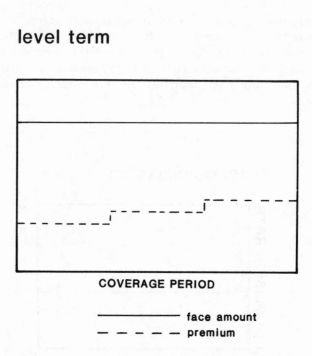

COVERAGE PERIOD

——————— **face amount**

— — — — — **premium**

liability (1) the exposure to risk, or actual experiencing of a loss. (2) the obligation to reimburse an injured person or the owner of damaged property. (3) a debt, or money owed by a company or person to another. Personal liabilities include mortgages and current debts. An insurance company's major liability is its policy reserves, representing the estimated present value of all future claims. See also *exposure to loss; loss; risk.*

liability insurance a form of insurance coverage protecting the insured against losses resulting from damage to property, bodily injury of another person as the result of acts or conditions in the insured's control, or damages awarded or settled in the event of a claim. See also *property and casualty insurance; risk.*

liability limits   the defined maximum dollar amount an insurance company will pay for losses under the terms of a policy. Limits include specifying covered and uncovered losses; time period during which any covered losses qualify for coverage; territorial coverage; dollar amounts; deductible and coinsurance exclusions; and legal versus illegal acts of the insured that result in losses. For example, under a liability policy, the insurance company will not pay losses under the following circumstances:

   — The loss is due to an earthquake, which is excluded from coverage.

   — The loss occurs one month after the policy has expired.

   — The loss occurs outside of the United States, and the policy specifies that it covers only domestic casualties.

   — The loss is greater than the maximum coverage provided; the excess will not be reimbursed.

   — The loss is not paid in full, due to reductions for deductible and coinsurance amounts.

   — The loss occurs while the insured was in the process of breaking the law.

See also *coverage; loss; risk.*

licensed agent   an insurance agent licensed to conduct business within the territorial limits of a state. Each state applies its own laws and regulations. In some cases, an individual with a professional designation may be granted a license without having to pass an examination; in other states, an individual may be granted a temporary license, pending an exam. See also *agent; broker.*

life annuity certain   an annuity with a specified number of payments, as a minimum. If the annuitant dies before all of the certain payments are made, payments will go to the benefiiciary. And if the annuitant lives beyond the certain period, payments will continue for life. See also *annuity certain; certain payment.* See illustration, page 114.

life contingency   a term describing the probability of an individual's living to a certain age; or that the individual will die at any specific age. On an average, a certain percentage of individuals will die at each given age. A life insurer must determine these probabilities to establish premiums and reserves for their policies. See also *mortality; probability.*

life estate   an interest in land that continues during the lifetime of one or more persons, and is contingent upon death or another specified event. Property can be put to any use the donee desires during his or her own lifetime. At death, that property reverts to the donor's estate. See also *estate planning.*

life annuity certain

| certain period |

| LIFE |
| PAYMENTS |

| LIFE |
| PAYMENTS |

---

life expectancy the statistical likelihood or probability of a person living to a specified age. When life insurance is purchased, the premium is established based on mortality information. See also *mortality; probability.*

life income descriptive of payments made to an annuitant under the provisions of an annuity with certain payments. See also *annuity; certain payment.*

life income with period certain one of several settlement options under a life insurance policy. The death benefit is converted to a life annuity, rather than being paid to the beneficiary in a lump sum. The insurer guarantees that payments will continue for a certain period. If the beneficiary (now the annuitant) dies before expiration of that period, the balance of those payments will be made to his or her named beneficiary. However, if the individual lives beyond the certain period, payments will continue for life. See also *annuity certain; certain payment; settlement option.*

---

life income with period certain

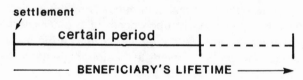

life income with refund   a provision included in the settlement option of a life insurance policy, in which monthly payments will continue for a minimum guaranteed period, or for as long as the individual lives. See also *settlement option.*

life insurance   protection against the economic loss resulting from the unexpected death of the insured. For example, a wage earner supports a family. In the event of that person's death, the family would suffer economically, and life insurance compensates for that loss.

Two major forms of life insurance include whole life and term. Whole life includes two parts: insurance and savings. During the period of coverage, each year's insurance portion decreases while the savings portion grows. The two, combined, always equal the face amount of the policy. At a specified future date, the insurance portion will be reduced to zero, and the entire policy will be owned by the insured as savings. At any time cash value is sufficient, the insured is allowed to borrow the savings portion through a policy loan. If the insured dies while a whole life insurance policy is in force, the entire face amount (minus any outstanding policy loans) is paid to the beneficiary.

Term insurance may be level or decreasing. A level term policy includes an unchanging face amount for a specified number of years. The policy can be renewed for the same face amount upon expiration of the term. However, premiums will be increased according to the insured's age. If the insured dies at any time during the term, the entire face amount is paid to the beneficiary. Decreasing term insurance includes a declining face amount over the term, with level premiums paid for the term. If the insured dies during the term, the current face amount is paid to the beneficiary.

Variations of these basic forms are sold widely, with combined fixed or variable savings and face value features built in as policy features. See also *beneficiary; death benefit; face amount; term life; variable life; whole life insurance.*

Life Insurance Association of America (LIAA)   a lobbying organization for the life insurance industry. See also *agent; broker; insurer.*

Life Insurance Marketing and Research Association (LIMRA)   an association that researches the problems of administering agency offices in the life insurance industry. See also *agency.*

life insurance trust   a trust established for the sole purpose of distributing life insurance proceeds upon the death of the insured. As part of an estate plan, for example, a policyowner establishes a trust to manage and pay out proceeds in the event that death occurs before his or her beneficiary reaches the age of 21. See also *beneficiary; estate planning; living trust; trust.*

Life Insurers Conference (LIC) an association of insurers that sells industrial, or debit insurance. It provides management information to member companies or agents. See also *debit insurance; industrial life; life insurance.*

Life Management Institute (LMI) an organization that, as part of the Life Office Management Association (LOMA), prepares and gives examinations to individuals seeking the FLMI designation. See also *Fellow, Life Management Institute (FLMI).*

Life Office Management Association (LOMA) an association that organizes study courses for members of the life insurance industry. See also *Fellow, Life Management Institute (FLMI); life insurance.*

life underwriter (1) an individual working in the home office of a life insurance company, who evaluates risks and investigates applications for insurance. (2) a life insurance agent. See also *agent; risk selection; underwriting.*

Life Underwriters Association (LUA) an association for life insurance agents that assists members with selling techniques and agency management. See also *agent.*

Life Underwriters Training Council (LUTC) an association supported by life insurance companies that offers sales training and techniques to member agents. See also *agent; life insurance.*

lifetime disability (1) a disability that is considered permanent, as defined in a disability income policy. (2) a benefit provided under some disability income policies, guaranteeing to make payments for the remainder of an insured's life, under certain circumstances. See also *benefit; disability benefit; permanent total disability.*

limited payment life whole life policies in which total premiums will be achieved by a point in the future. The policy is paid up at that point, even though it can be continued in force beyond the paid up date. For example, an insured buys a policy calling for payments for 20 years. At the end of that term, premiums cease. The full face value will be paid to a beneficiary at any time before or after that date. See also *fully paid; life insurance; whole life insurance.* See illustration, page 117.

limited payment life

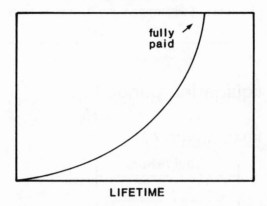

LIFETIME

---

line of insurance   one of five major classifications of insurance available to businesses, individuals or groups. The five lines are:

1. Life insurance—protection against the economic consequences of the insured's death.

2. Health insurance—protection in the event of medical expenses beyond the deductible and coinsurance limits; hospitalization protection, or payments of hospital bills while the insured is a patient; or disability income payments in the event the insured is partially or totally disabled.

3. Property and casualty insurance—protection against catastrophic losses to property due to fire, weather, theft, vandalism and other causes.

4. Liability insurance—protection against losses of property or injuries to other persons, resulting from claims due to acts of the insured.

5. Annuities—not strictly insurance, these are programs designed to provide individuals with periodic payments (annuity benefits) for life or for a specified (certain) period of time.

See also *annuity; health insurance; liability insurance; life insurance; property and casualty insurance.*

liquidation fee   the fee charged to an annuitant for withdrawal from the annuity plan. The fee reimburses the insurer for underwriting the risk—which is designed for the long-term—and also serves as an incentive not to cancel or withdraw from the plan. See also *annuity; termination.*

liquidation period   the period of time that an annuitant will actually receive benefits. Under the provisions of a pure annuity, the liquidation period is defined as the lifetime of the annuitant. Under a refund annuity, the liquidation period is the greater of a guaranteed period of time, or the lifetime of the annuitant. See also *annuity; pure annuity; refund annuity.*

liquidation period

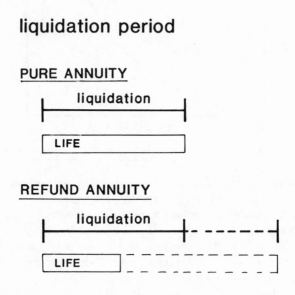

living benefits insurance provisions that the insured has while still living. These include the right to take out a policy loan to the extent of current cash value; the right to disability income; Waiver of Premium (WP) when that coverage is part of the policy; and the right to surrender a policy and receive current cash value. See also *cash value; disability income; policy loan; surrender value; Waiver of Premium (WP).*

living trust a trust that exists or is established while the grantor is living, and will go into effect during the grantor's lifetime. In comparison, a testamentary trust is one designed to take effect upon the death of the grantor. See also *inter-vivos trust; testamentary trust; trust.*

living will a will stipulating the individual's wishes in the event that death is a certainty. For example, the individual states in a living will that no heroic measures are to be taken after a terminal injury, and that life is not to be prolonged by any artificial means. See also *will.*

load the amount of additional premium added to the net premium, to pay for the agent's commission, and for the insurance company's cost of marketing, administration, and product development. See also *commission; gross premium; net premium; no-load.*

loan value the amount currently available in the form of cash value. Under the provisions of a whole life insurance policy, the policyowner can borrow the loan value at any time. See also *cash value; life insurance; policy loan; whole life insurance.*

long-tail liability a liability that occurs in one time period and manifests itself later. The term describes the problem being faced by insurers today. Under one theory, the occurrence injury theory, an insurer is liable for losses that occur only if a policy was in force during the period an injury occurred. A conflicting theory, the manifestation injury theory, holds that an insurer is liable for all losses, even those that occurred before coverage began, as long as the problem is manifested during the policy period. See also *manifestation injury theory; occurrence injury theory.*

long-tail liability

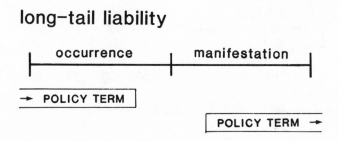

long-term disability a disability that exceeds a specified period of time. The actual number of days or months considered as "long-term" will vary by company. Some insurers consider six months or more as a long-term period. Others define it as a disability lasting five years or more. In some companies, long-term has the same meaning as "permanent." In others, a long-term disability is not necessarily permanent. Coverages may specify different levels of payment for long-term liability, as opposed to payments that will be made for a limited period of time. Most policies also set a maximum number of years that benefits will continue. See also *disability income; income replacement; integration.*

loss   the experienced reduction of value, partial or complete, for which an insured places a claim with the insurance company. The contract of insurance will specify that the company will pay the amount of the loss up to the limits of coverage, its share of coinsurance, or a pro rata distribution amount. See also *claim; coinsurance; coverage; pro rata distribution; risk.*

loss clause   that section of the insurance contract that explains how losses are computed, and what limits are placed on actual payments. Limits for covered losses are limited in three ways: by deductibles, coinsurance, and maximums.

Example: A policy specifies a $2,000 deductible and a 20% coinsurance rate. The maximum loss the company will pay is $50,000. Two policyholders have losses, in the amounts of $75,000 and $30,000. The loss payments will be:

	Case 1	Case 2
Total loss	$75,000	$30,000
less: deductible	2,000	2,000
Sub-total	$73,000	$28,000
Less: 20% coinsurance	14,600	5,600
Sub-total	$58,400	$22,400
Less: amount over max.	8,400	−0−
Loss paid	$50,000	$22,400

See also *coinsurance; deductible; liability; property and casualty insurance; risk.* See illustration, page 121.

Loss Frequency Method (LFM)   a method used to estimate the cost of losses in the future. This is used to calculate required premium and reserve levels or adjustments. See also *load; net premium; premium; reserve.*

loss prevention   a technique of risk management, the purpose of which is to reduce the cost of insurance by reducing the chances of loss. For individuals, loss prevention can include elimination of fire hazards, installing fire or burglar alarms, and safety maintenance of automobiles. For businesses, preventive measures include safety programs, elimination of dangerous materials and conditions, and providing employees incentives for positive safety records on the job. See also *risk management.*

loss clause

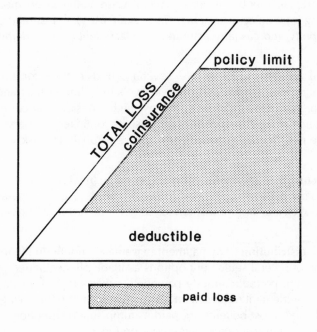

Loss Ratio Reserve Method (LRRM)   a formula for calculating reserve requirements for a specific line of insurance, used in the property and casualty industry. Earned premium volume is compared to the trend in losses and related expenses, so that reserve levels can be adjusted. See also *property and casualty insurance; reserve.*

loss reserves   reserves established to estimate the pending losses to be paid. These losses include a provision for Incurred But Not Reported (IBNR) losses, existing and known claims that have not yet been paid to policyowners, claims acknowledged but not due until a future date, or losses reported in the end of one period but not paid until the next. The reserve can also include a contingency for contingent losses that will not be manifested for many years, but that the company expects to have to pay. See also *claim; Incurred But Not Reported (IBNR); reserve.*

loss settlement   the method or procedure for paying losses to the insured or to a beneficiary. This includes loss payment limits and provisions for deductibles, coinsurance and policy maximums, as well as the distinction between replacement cost versus Actual Cash Value (ACV) methods for computing losses. See also *Actual Cash Value (ACV); coinsurance; deductible; property and casualty insurance; replacement cost; settlement.*

loss trend analysis of losses over several periods of time, for the purpose of evaluating profitability and reserve levels for a line of insurance. If the trend is highly unfavorable, a company might consider not continuing to offer that line of coverage; or must increase its contingency reserve to cover the future risk. See also *contingency reserve; probability; risk.*

losses incurred a measurement of experience, in which the actual losses the company pays are compared to the premium income generated for a class of policies or line of insurance. See also *incurred loss; reserve.*

lump sum distribution any payment in a single amount. In life insurance, this is one of several settlement options available. Beneficiaries can select the lump sum, periodic annuity payments, other forms of insurance, and varieties of settlement modes. If an alternative method of receiving benefits is not selected, most benefits are paid as lump sum distributions. See also *death benefit; life insurance; settlement option.*

M

McCarran Act federal legislation enacted in 1945, as a result of the 1942 case *United States versus South-Eastern Underwriters Association.* In that case, the government contended that companies participating together as South-Eastern were in violation of the Sherman Antitrust Act and, in 1944, the U.S. Supreme Court agreed. This raised questions about the states' ability to regulate activities of insurance companies. The National Association of Insurance Commissioners (NAIC) proposed a series of rules that would allow insurance companies to remain exempt from the Sherman Antitrust Act on the condition that each state maintain regulatory standards. The resulting law, introduced by Nevada Senator McCarran, is also known as Public Law 15 and is part of Title 15, Commerce and Trade Code. It exempts insurance companies from the Sherman Antitrust Act, the Clayton Act and the Federal Trade Commission Act—federal anti-monopoly laws. The most significant segment of that law is a statement in Section 1012:

"The business of insurance, and every person engaged therein, shall be subject to the laws of the several states which relate to the regulation or taxation of such business."

As a result of Public Law 15, insurance companies are regulated on the state level. See also *National Association of Insurance Commissioners (NAIC)*.

major hospitalization   a specialized form of health insurance that pays expenses of the insured that are incurred while in the hospital. Policy features include a deductible, a coinsurance clause, and an identification of the maximum amount that can be paid out under the terms of the policy. See also *coinsurance; deductible; health insurance*.

major medical   health insurance designed to protect the insured against the economic consequences of a catastrophic illness. Once a medical insurance plan's limits have been met, a major medical plan's benefits begin. Coverage includes hospital expenses, drugs and medicines, and special treatments. In some policies, major medical is identical to hospitalization plans. In others, it does not restrict covered expenses just to those incurred while a patient. See also *coinsurance; comprehensive major medical; deductible; health insurance*.

malpractice liability   insurance for professionals who risk substantial losses in the event of a malpractice suit. Doctors, dentists, accountants and attorneys, for example, pay substantial premiums for protection against the contingent losses from lawsuits. The policy includes provisions for legal defense against claims, and will pay damages up to a stated maximum. See also *liability insurance; professional liability insurance*.

Mandatory Securities Valuation Reserve (MSVR)   a reserve established by life insurance companies to provide for possible losses in an investment portfolio. The MSVR, required by the National Association of Insurance Commissioners (NAIC), sets guidelines for the percentage of each type of security that must be reserved. Example: the NAIC guidelines state that a certain type of security must set aside 5% of current market value in the MSVR. At the end of the year, that security is valued at $35,000. The company must adjust its MSVR to a value of $1,750, to allow for possible losses in value. See also *life insurance; reserve*.

manifestation injury theory   a theory contending that an insurer is liable for payment of claims on a policy only for the period during which an injury becomes known. Example: An individual was exposed to a hazard many years ago, when he had a policy with insurer A. Now, it's discovered that the individual was injured due to that exposure. His policy is currently with insurer B. Under the manifestation injury theory, insurer B is liable for claims resulting from that injury. See also *long-tail liability; occurrence injury theory.*

manual rate   the rate per $1,000 of insurance charged for a standard risk (life insurance), or the cost per unit of insurance (property and casualty). It is called the "manual" rate because those rates are published in a rating book, or manual. See also *life insurance; property and casualty insurance; rate making; standard risk.*

marine insurance   protection against damage, theft and other losses to goods while in transit. Marine insurance policies are in effect while goods are transported over waters (ocean marine) or over land (inland marine). See also *casualty insurance; inland marine; ocean marine.*

market value clause   a section of a property and casualty policy stating that reimbursement of losses will be made on the basis of current market value, rather than based on cost. Under the Actual Cash Value (ACV) method, the insured is entitled to reimbursement of the original cost of property, minus depreciation. The market value clause specifies that the replacement cost method will be used to calculate the value of property. The claim will equal the amount that a willing buyer would pay to a willing seller. However, the replacement cost often is limited to a specified percentage of value as calculated under the ACV method. Example: An asset originally cost $15,000, but its current market value is $17,000. Under the ACV method, the depreciated value is $3,000, and the policy stipulates that the maximum reimbursement is limited to 400% of ACV. Even though current market value is $17,000, the amount the insurer will reimburse is $12,000 (ACV value of $3,000, multiplied by 400%). See also *Actual Cash Value (ACV); casualty insurance; property and casualty insurance; replacement cost.*

mass underwriting   the setting of rates and risk limitations of a group of individuals, rather than on the basis of each person's age, health, sex, or other factors. Example: A company issues individual policies, and will underwrite on the basis on each person's application. It also issues health insurance, based on the characteristics of the group as a whole (average age, geographic region, type of work, etc.). Mass underwriting is practical when the group has something in common, such as working for the same employer. See also *group contract; underwriting.*

master policy   in group insurance, the contract issued to the employer or administrator of the group. Each individual participating in the policy is given a certificate that explains benefits in an abbreviated form. See also *eligible employee; group contract.*

---

master policy

---

master-servant rule   a premise in agency law stating that the employer or principal is liable for the negligent acts of the employee or agent. See also *agency; liability; negligence.*

maturity date   the date when proceeds of an endowment become payable to the insured person. For example, premium payments are made for 20 years on a $50,000 endowment. During that time, in the event of the death of the insured, the beneficiary will receive payment of the entire face amount. At the maturity date, the entire $50,000 is payable to the insured. See also *endowment; life insurance.*

---

maturity date

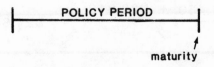

maturity dividend an extra dividend paid to the owner of a participating policy, paid when the policy matures. See also *dividend; extra dividend; life insurance; participating policy.*

maturity value the face amount of an endowment or whole life policy. It will be paid upon the death of the insured or upon maturity date if the insured is still living. See also *endowment; face amount; life insurance; whole life insurance.*

Maximum Foreseeable Loss (MFL) the highest possible loss that can occur to property covered under a casualty insurance policy. Example: A home is insured under a policy. The MFL is a total loss of the home and all property, excluding the value of land. See also *casualty insurance.*

Maximum Probable Loss (MPL) the highest likely loss that will occur to property covered under a casualty insurance policy. Example: A home is insured under a policy, but a fire department station is situated across the street. The MPL is lower than a total loss, due to the proximity of the station and the ability to respond immediately. See also *casualty insurance.*

mean reserve the legal reserve for each policy of insurance. It is the average of each year's initial and terminal reserves. Example: One policy's initial year reserve is $21,450, and its terminal reserve is $22,318. The mean (average) is $21,884. This is the amount the company is required to establish as a reserve liability for the year, for that policy. See also *initial reserve; legal reserve; reserve; terminal reserve.*

---

mean reserve

$$\frac{\text{initial reserve} \ + \ \text{terminal reserve}}{2}$$

$$\frac{\$21,450 \ + \ \$22,318}{2} \ = \ \$21,884$$

median   the central value in a field of numbers, used in statistics to identify points of probability. Example: A number of insurance policies on the books of a company represent various levels of risk. To compute the typical probable loss, the actuary calculates both the average risk and the median risk. See also *actuarial adjustments; expected mortality; probability; risk.*

Medicaid   a provision providing welfare benefits to low-income individuals, also referred to as Title XIX of the Social Security amendments of 1965. Benefits are computed on a sliding scale based on family income. See also *Social Security Act of 1935.*

medical examination   a requirement imposed on certain individuals applying for life or health insurance. The decision to require a medical exam depends on the age of the applicant, the amount of insurance applied for, and the experience of the insurance company. Based on the physician's report, the company may issue a standard policy; issue a rated policy for substandard risks; or decline to provide insurance on any basis. See also *adverse selection; health insurance; life insurance; risk selection; underwriting.*

Medical Information Bureau (MIB)   an organization that collects health information on individuals who have applied for life and health insurance. Upon receiving an applicant, a company requests a report from MIB, to discover any unreported conditions. See also *adverse selection; health insurance; life insurance.*

Medicare   Title XVIII of the Social Security amendments of 1965, providing medical benefit payments for individuals over the age of 65 and those under 65 who are disabled. The benefit is provided by way of payroll deductions, and includes two parts: hospital insurance and supplementary medical insurance. See also *health insurance; hospitalization insurance; Social Security Act of 1935.*

medigap   forms of insurance designed to pay the portion of medical and hospitalization not covered under the Medicare program. See also *health insurance.*

merit rating   a system of varying premiums under a plan of insurance, based on the loss experience to the company. See also *experience modification; loss.*

Million Dollar Round Table (MDRT)   an association whose members include life insurance agents who have sold specified levels of insurance during a single year. The actual amount is adjusted each year based on changes in the cost of living. See also *agent; life insurance.*

minimum benefit the smallest amount of insurance coverage a company is willing to underwrite. The minimum is set to justify the company's administrative costs per policy. See also *face amount; life insurance.*

minimum deposit whole life a form of whole life insurance in which an initial deposit provides cash value. This is to be used to pay future premiums with policy loans. The original premise was to establish tax-deductible interest expenses in a largely self-funded insurance program. However, tax legislation has eliminated the deductibility of interest of this type. See also *cash value; deposit premium; life insurance; policy loan; whole life insurance.*

minimum group the smallest number of people required to form a legitimate group, as established by state law, the insurer, or both. See also *group contract.*

minimum premium **(1)** the smallest dollar amount an insurer will accept as modal premium. Example: A relatively small life insurance policy is set up for either semiannual or annual premium payments. The company will not allow the insured to pay quarterly or monthly, because those payments would be smaller than the minimum premium. **(2)** the smallest amount of gross premium a company will charge for a policy, based on requirements for administration and placing that policy in the records of the company. **(3)** the fee charged by an insurer to a self-insured group, to administer claims. See also *modal premium; premium.*

minimum standards the definition of what an insurance company considers an insurable risk. For example, a company specifies that individuals will qualify for insurance if they do not pursue dangerous hobbies, work in hazardous occupations, or have terminal illnesses. See also *insurable risk; risk selection.*

mixed company an insurance company combining features of mutual and stock companies. A mutual company is one owned entirely by policyholders, who receive proportionate shares of profits each year. A stock company is a corporation owned by stockholders. A mixed company sells both participating and non-participating policies, so that a portion of ownership is mutual and a portion is stock. See also *mutual company; stock company.*

mobile home policy   a policy providing liability and casualty protection to owners of mobile homes, similar to coverage provided under a homeowner's policy. The difference, though, is that a mobile home is not real estate, but personal property. See also *homeowner's insurance; personal property.*

modal premium   the method of payment of the annual premium. There are four types:

Annual mode—a single annual payment.

Semiannual mode—two payments per year.

Quarterly mode—four payments per year.

Monthly mode—12 payments per year, most often by way of automatic deductions from bank accounts.

Modes other than the annual are often increased for a service charge. Policyholders can change the mode as they please, assuming the insurer has not placed restrictions as part of the policy contract.

Example: A policy's premium is $200 per year. Before computing service charges, modal premium will be one of the following: $200 (annual); $100 (semiannual); $50 (quarterly); or $16.67 (monthly). See also *annual premium; premium.*

---

modal premium

ANNUALLY

$$\frac{\$200}{1} = \$200$$

QUARTERLY

$$\frac{\$200}{4} = \$50$$

SEMIANNUALLY

$$\frac{\$200}{2} = \$100$$

MONTHLY

$$\frac{\$200}{12} = \$16.67$$

mode method of paying an insurance premium. The mode often is determined by the policyholder's preference. Payments are made annually, semiannually, quarterly, or monthly. See also *premium*.

modification rate an adjustment to the annual premium, based on the loss experience of a single policy, or of a range of similar coverages, also called the merit rating. See also *experience modification; merit rating*.

modified cash refund annuity a form of annuity that promises to repay a specific amount of cash to the annuitant (or to the employee when the annuity is used to fund a retirement program). In the event the annuitant dies before that amount has been repaid, the balance will be paid to the beneficiary. See also *annuity; cash refund annuity; refund annuity*.

modified cash refund annuity

ANNUITIZATION

guaranteed payments

modified coinsurance a form of reinsurance agreement in which the original (ceding) company retains the entire reserve and all premiums, and makes annual adjustments with the reinsurance company. In this usage, the term coinsurance refers to an agreement to jointly insure a risk, rather than to the sharing of risks between the insurance company and the insured. See also *coinsurance; reinsurance*.

modified life a form of whole life insurance in which premiums for a limited number of years are somewhat higher than rates for term insurance. After expiration of that term, premiums are adjusted to a level slightly higher than rates for whole life. The purpose is to attract policyholders who want to build cash value, but who cannot afford the premium that would be required under the usual policy. Cash value does not build significantly during the first few years; but the policyholder is more likely to be able to afford higher rates in the future. See also *cash value; graded premium; life insurance; whole life insurance*. See illustration, page 131.

modified life

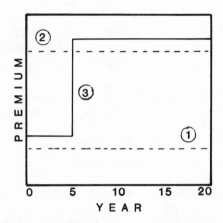

1 - comparable term insurance
rate

2 - ordinary whole life
insurance rate

3 - modified life rate

---

modified reserves   reserves that have been altered due to the method of collecting premiums. See also *net level premium reserve; reserve.*

money damages   awards given to plaintiffs in a liability suit, or paid out as settlement of a claim. Money damages are of two types: compensatory damages, payments for expenses actually incurred; and punitive damages, intended to punish the defendant for negligent acts. See also *liability; negligence.*

money purchase plan   a form of pension plan in which contributions by the employer are made on a fixed formula. Upon retirement, each plan employee receives benefits on the basis of relative participation in the plan. See also *defined contribution plan; pension plan.*

Monthly Debit Ordinary (MDO)   a form of life insurance designed for collection by the agent of a monthly premium. See also *debit insurance; life insurance; ordinary life.*

morbidity the frequency and severity of illness, used to set rates and estimate claims in health insurance policies. See also *accident and health; severity rate.*

morbidity rate the likelihood of claims under health insurance plans, based on historical trends by age, sex, geographic region, or for members of an identified group. See also *accident and health; loss trend; severity rate.*

morbidity table a table listing for each age and sex the frequency and severity of health insurance claims. See also *probability; severity rate.*

mortality the measurement of the number of deaths that will occur, on average, at any given age. See also *death rate.*

mortality adjustment the calculation of mortality for an individual or group of individuals, in comparison to mortality rates for a larger group. Such adjustments might be necessary due to trends by region, for example. See also *death rate; loss trend.*

mortality rate the likelihood of death at a given age, based on historical information for a large group of individuals. See also *death rate; loss trend.*

mortality table a table reporting the average rate of death for each given age, based on studies of a large group of individuals over many years. See also *death rate; probability.*

mortgage insurance insurance on an individual's life or health, the benefit amount of which is tied to the amount payable on a home mortgage. There are three broad types:

mortgage life—the face amount is the principal amount of the mortgage. Over time, as the mortgage is paid down, the amount of insurance in force also declines. This is a form of decreasing term life. In the event of the insured's death, the insurance company will pay off the entire mortgage balance.

joint mortgage life—the coverage is the same as that for mortgage life, but coverage extends to both husband and wife under a single policy. In the event of the death of either spouse, the entire mortgage balance will be paid by the insurance company. This coverage is appropriate for two-income families, especially when the family could not afford to continue mortgage payments in the event one of the incomes ceased.

mortgage disability—the benefit is identical to the amount of monthly mortgage payment. In the event the insured is disabled, the insurance company will continue to make mortgage payments to the lender. During the period of disability, continuing premiums are commonly waived as well.

See also *decreasing term life; disability income; face amount; life insurance.*

Moving Average Rating Method (MARM)   a system for projecting future losses on an average, so that premiums will be adequate to pay claims without the need for adjustment. The calculation must involve a combination of factors, including actual loss experience, the factor of adverse selection, and investment income the company expects to earn over a period of years. See also *adverse selection; life insurance; loss.*

Moving Average Rating Method (MARM)

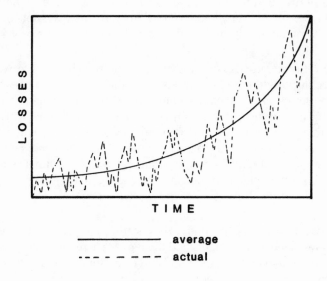

T I M E

————————— **average**

- - - — — - - **actual**

Multiple Employer Trust (MET)   a trust formed by several companies to provide group health benefits, either as a plan of self-insurance or to obtain a single group policy underwritten by an insurance company. Example: Several employers agree to form a MET and make monthly payments to the trust. All health claims submitted by eligible employees are to be paid from the common pool. Example: Several employers form a MET and each contributes a proportionate share of a single monthly premium. The premium is then paid to an insurer who provides group health benefits through a single master policy. See also *group health; self-insurance; trust.*

multiple lines   the carrying of more than one type of insurance by a company, or selling of several lines of insurance by one agency. Example: Some agencies specialize in only one form of insurance, such as life or health. Others carry multiple lines, such as life, health, homeowner's, and property and casualty. See also *line of insurance.*

multiple location form   insurance on individuals or property in more than one location. Example: A single policy can be written to cover the property of one employer with several stores or warehouses. Or, one individual is insured while at a place of employment, even though that person visits several offices per week. See also *property and casualty insurance.*

multiple perils   descriptive of a single policy that defines a number of different types of losses covered, even when those losses are not commonly included in one policy form. See also *casualty insurance; umbrella policy.*

multiple retirement ages   classifications of the possible ages at which an employee decides to retire, and the benefits that will be paid in each case, under the terms of a retirement plan. The normal retirement age is the earliest age an employee can usually retire to receive full benefits. The early retirement age is the age at which an employee has met requirements for years of service. Retiring at this age usually involves a reduced benefit amount. A deferred retirement age is any age beyond normal retirement, and could result in increased benefits, depending on terms specified in the plan. See also *normal retirement age; retirement age.*

mutual assent   a concept in contract law, stating that a contract is valid only if both sides agree to and understand the terms. There must be an offer and acceptance, or a meeting of the minds, in order for a contract to exist. See also *acceptance; contract; offer.*

mutual company   a type of insurance company that is owned entirely by the policyholders, in proportionate shares. A managing board is elected by the policyholders to manage and direct the company. In comparison, a stock company is a corporation with shares of stock, and ownership is determined by who purchases and holds those shares. In a mutual company, all profits are distributed to policyholders through policy dividends. See also *dividend; stock company.*

N

named insured   the individual or company whose life, health or property is insured in a specific policy. The insured is not necessarily the same person as the policyholder. See also *insured; policyholder.*

named perils   those specific perils that are covered in a property and casualty policy. All perils not named are excluded. In an all risks policy, all perils are covered except named exclusions. Homeowner insurance policies are available in two forms of named peril coverages—one naming 11 common perils, and another specifying 18 perils. These are:
Eleven named perils:
1. Fire or lightning
2. Loss of property removed from premises due to danger from fire or other perils
3. Windstorm or hail
4. Explosion
5. Riot or civil commotion
6. Aircraft
7. Vehicles
8. Smoke
9. Vandalism and malicious mischief
10. Theft
11. Breakage of glass that is a part of a building
Extended coverage:
12. Falling objects
13. Weight of ice, snow or sleet
14. Collapse of buildings or building parts
15. Sudden and accidental tearing, cracking, burning or bulging of a steam or hot water heating system
16. Accidental discharge, leakage or overflow from plumbing, heating or air conditioning systems or domestic appliances
17. Freezing of plumbing, heating or air conditioning systems and domestic appliances
18. Sudden and accidental injury from artificially generated currents to electrical appliances, fixtures or wiring
See also *all risks; exclusion; property and casualty insurance.*

National Association of Independent Insurance Adjusters (NAIIA)   a trade association whose members are independent claims adjusters. See also *adjuster; claim.*

National Association of Insurance Agents (NAIA) a trade association for insurance agents, whose membership consists primarily of property and casualty independent agents. See also *agent; independent agent.*

National Association of Insurance Brokers (NAIB) an association for insurance brokers, that provides industry information to its membership. See also *broker.*

National Association of Insurance Commissioners (NAIC) an association of state insurance commissioners, whose function is to ensure adequate regulation of the insurance industry. Formed as part of the legislative changes brought about by the McCarran Act, enabling the various states to regulate insurers, the NAIC strives for uniform standards. It has established:
- —a convention blank, a uniform report that every insurer files annually to disclose financial information
- —reserve valuation standards
- —guidelines for the valuation of securities held in insurers' portfolios
- —standardization of nonforfeiture benefits

Each state's Commissioner of Insurance, in addition to its regulation and compliance with uniform standards in the industry, serves as a consumer protection agency, and hears consumer complaints or addresses inquiries concerning the activities of companies and agencies operating in each state. See also *Commissioner of Insurance; McCarran Act; statutory requirements.*

National Association of Life Companies (NALC) an association whose members are life and health insurance companies. See also *health insurance; life insurance.*

National Association of Life Underwriters (NALU) a major trade association of life and health insurance agents. The association offers regional and national seminars and conventions, and promotes ethics in agency practices. See also *agent; health insurance; life insurance.*

National Council on Compensation Insurance (NCCI) an organization comprised of member insurers who provide workers compensation coverage. The association provides statistical information, and files rate plans with state insurance commissioners. See also *workers compensation.*

National Flood Insurance Program (NFIP) a federal program enacted as part of the 1968 National Flood Act. Participating insurers provide homeowners and business owners with flood insurance, through a nationally organized insurance pool. See also *casualty insurance; property and casualty insurance.*

National Flood Insurers Association (NFIA)   an association that provided a pool for participating insurance companies, prior to enactment of the National Flood Act in 1968. See also *casualty insurance; property and casualty insurance.*

National Insurance Association (NIA)   an organization that provides members with an exchange of ideas and information, particularly for the concerns of providing small business liability and individual lines of insurance. See also *business liability.*

National Insurance Development Corporation (NIDC)   a government-sponsored organization that assists insurers in reinsuring the risks of riot and civil commotion insurance, brought about when many companies chose to no longer assume the risks of this line of insurance. See also *reinsurance.*

National Insurance Producers Conference (NIPC)   a trade association whose members are agents and brokers, primarily independent agents. See also *agent; broker; independent agent.*

National Service Life Insurance (NSLI)   a program of government life insurance active from the 1940s until 1950. Policies still in force ensure participants' lives in amounts from $1,000 to $10,000, as renewable term life insurance. See also *government life insurance.*

natural group   as defined for the purpose of qualifying for group insurance, any group that shares something in common and was formed for a purpose other than to obtain insurance. Factors in common may include the same employer, or membership in a professional or fraternal group, credit union, or other association. Most insurers further specify that the group must be in existence for a minimum period of time to be considered a natural group. See also *group contract.*

natural loss   any loss caused by nature, beyond the control or anticipation of humans. See also *act of God; casualty insurance; property and casualty insurance.*

needs approach   a procedure used in financial, estate and retirement planning. It involves analysis of an individual's specific needs, considering family support and current or future income requirements. Aspects include the need for current income, continued income in the event of death, disability or poor health of a family's wage earner, ongoing liabilities (such as a home mortgage), future expenses (college education of children, for example), retirement needs, and estate planning. See also *estate planning; financial plan; retirement plan.*

negligence the failure to use an appropriate degree of care or to act as a reasonable person would act in a given set of circumstances. See also *liability; tort law.*

net amount at risk the amount of a life insurance death benefit that is greater than the policy's terminal reserve. For example, of all policies sold, a portion are assumed to result in claims each year. Policies are established at a level adequate to pay all future claims. However, some policies will result in claims greater than the amount of established reserves. The difference between the maximum death benefit and the reserve at the end of that year is the amount at risk. See also *death benefit; life insurance; risk; terminal reserve.*

net amount at risk

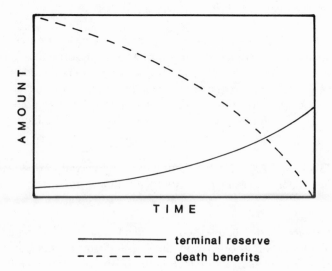

TIME

——————— terminal reserve

– – – – – – – death benefits

net interest earned   the average amount of interest an insurance company earns on its portfolio of securities, after deducting investment expenses. See also *investment income.*

Net Level Premium (NLP)   premium charged on a life insurance policy that remains unchanged throughout the period it is in force. The net premium is the pure cost of mortality. See also *life insurance.*

Net Level Premium (NLP)

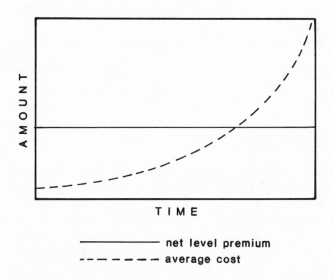

net level premium
average cost

net level premium reserve   reserve to pay all future claims, under the net level premium system. It is assumed that the present value of all future premiums will equal the present value of all future benefits, if the reserve is calculated accurately. Policyholders overpay during the early years of coverage (on average), and underpay during the later years. See also *benefit; premium; present value; reserve.* See illustration, page 140.

net payments index   an analysis of average, or relative costs for groups of cash value insurance policies, based on the net cost method, as opposed to the Interest Adjusted Cost (IAC) method. See also *cash value; Interest Adjusted Cost (IAC).*

net level premium reserve

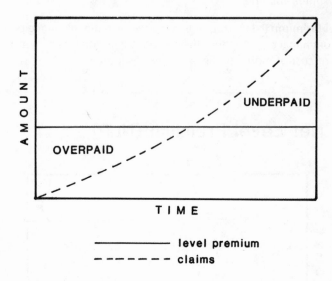

OVERPAID

UNDERPAID

AMOUNT

T I M E

————————— level premium
— — — — — — claims

---

net premium the amount of premium charged on a particular type of policy, assuming the company will earn a specified rate of interest during the average policy term, and based on assumptions of the mortality rate at each age of issue. The net premium is calculated before an added loan for agent commissions and administrative costs to the company, used to arrive at the gross premium. See also *gross premium; load; mortality rate; premium.*

net single premium a form of payment for a policy, in which the insured makes one payment at the beginning of the insurance or annuity term. The future benefit is paid (a) at the end of the insurance period, or (b) during the period of annuitization. See also *annuity; premium; single premium life.* See illustration, page 141.

net worth the value of an organization, or an individual's property value, consisting of all assets, minus all liabilities. An insurance company must report its net worth each year on its convention blank. Certain assets are non-admitted, and cannot be considered in calculating net worth on a statutory basis. See also *convention blank; statutory requirements.*

new business insurance business generated during the last 12 months, or during a calendar year. All first-year business is the basis for the majority of

net single premium

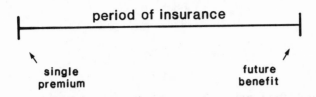

period of insurance

**single
premium**

**future
benefit**

---

life insurance agents' commissions, since first-year rates (based on new business written) are substantially greater than renewal rates. The distinction of new business versus existing policy risks is important to the insurance company as well, in evaluating trends, and because initial costs are greater for new business during the first year. See also *first year commission; life insurance.*

no-fault a concept in property and casualty insurance, especially for automobile coverages, in which liability is insured without assigning fault to one driver or another. Both bodily injury and property damages are covered under the policy, and certain restrictions are placed on claims for damages by injured motorists. See also *automobile insurance; liability insurance; property and casualty insurance.*

no-load insurance sold without any load for the agent's commission or for administrative expenses of the company or a broker. Some forms of insurance promoted as no-load are actually back-load policies, charging a fee in future years rather than in the first year; others assess service charges each year, and are not pure no-load policies. See also *back-end load; front-end load; load.*

nominal interest rate the stated rate of interest, without regard for the method of compounding that will be in effect. For example, the rate of 8.00% is quoted as a guaranteed rate. If compounding takes place monthly, the annual interest rate will be 8.30%; if quarterly, the annual rate will be 8.24%; and if semiannually, the annual rate will be 8.16%.
    Compound rates are computed as:

$$1 + \left(\frac{R}{P}\right)^{P}$$

R = rate   P = periods

Example: To compute quarterly compounding of 8.00%, first divide the rate by the number of periods in the year (4):

$$\frac{.08}{4} = .02$$

Add 1:

$$.02 + 1 = 1.02$$

Now multiply the result by itself four times (for the number of periods):

$$1.02 \times 1.02 \times 1.02 \times 1.02 = 1.0824$$

Next, drop the '1', and the balance is the annual rate when compounded quarterly—8.24%.

To compute monthly compound interest, use 12 periods after dividing the rate by 12; and for semi-annual, use two periods after dividing the rate by two. See also *compound interest; interest rate; investment income.*

---

nominal interest rate

NOMINAL RATE	COMPOUND METHOD		
	MONTHLY	QUARTERLY	SEMI-ANNUALLY
7.00%	7.23%	7.19%	7.12%
8.00	8.30	8.24	8.16
9.00	9.38	9.31	9.20
10.00	11.05	11.04	10.25

---

non-admitted assets assets of an insurance company that cannot be counted as part of net worth, under statutory rules. Assets that must be considered as non-admitted include agents' debit balances (money agents owe to the company for advances against future commissions), and furniture and fixtures. See also *admitted assets; convention blank; GAAP requirements; statutory requirements.*

non-admitted company   an insurer who is not licensed to conduct business in a specific state. See also *domestic company; foreign company.*

non-admitted reinsurance   reinsurance credits due to a company that cannot be paid, because the company is not admitted to conduct business in the applicable state. See also *admitted company; reinsurance.*

noncancellable guaranteed renewable   more often referred to simply as noncancellable, health insurance policies on which the insurer, by contract, cannot cancel the policy during an agreed-upon term, and cannot change the premium rate. Upon expiration of the term, the insured has the right to renew the policy under the same conditions. See also *guaranteed renewable; health insurance; renewal clause.*

nonforfeiture option   one of four methods a policyholder may select when premium payments cease. The cash value is not forfeited, but is applied in one of these ways:
1. Surrender the policy and receive full cash value.
2. Take out a loan up to the full amount of current cash value.
3. Purchase paid-up term insurance, using cash value for the single premium.
4. Purchase extended term insurance, for as long a period of time possible with the current level of cash value.

See also *cash value; extended term; life insurance; optional settlement mode; paid-up insurance; policy loan; surrender value.*

nonforfeiture provision   a clause in every whole life or endowment policy sold in the United States, specifying that cash value cannot be forfeited by the policyowner as a consequence on non-payment of premiums. See also *endowment; life insurance; optional settlement mode; whole life insurance.*

non-medical limit   the maximum amount of life insurance a company will allow on a single policy without requiring a medical examination from the applicant. This is a safeguard against adverse selection, the tendency of an individual to seek insurance with knowledge of a medical problem. The limit protects the company against losses that would occur above and beyond the expected mortality for a given age. See also *adverse selection; expected mortality; life insurance; medical examination; risk selection; underwriting.*

non-occupational disability   a disability that occurs due to factors not related to the workplace. Work-related injuries are insured through mandatory workers compensation policies. However, additional coverage may be desirable to protect against the economic consequences of non-occupational injuries. See also *disability benefit; workers compensation.*

non-participating policy a life insurance policy in which the policyowner is not entitled to dividends. See also *dividend; life insurance; participating policy.*

non-qualified plan a form of retirement or incentive plan that does not qualify for tax deferred treatment. Because contributions and earnings are taxed each year, the potential compound value of such a plan is substantially lower than a comparable qualified plan. However, under a non-qualified plan, employers are not limited to the restrictive rules concerning discrimination, and may provide value incentives to employees as they choose. See also *qualified plan; retirement plan; tax deferral.*

normal annuity form a retirement plan that establishes an annuity program for employees, and whose premiums are calculated on the assumption that the individual will begin to take benefits as of normal retirement age. In the event of early retirement, participating employees will receive a recalculated, reduced benefit. See also *annuity; retirement age.*

normal retirement age the age at which employees may retire and still receive maximum benefits under the agreed-upon terms of a retirement plan. The plan specifies the amount of benefit possible if an employee retires before that age, and also sets a limit on the computation of benefits for those retiring later than the normal retirement age. See also *multiple retirement ages; retirement plan.*

notice of cancellation a document advising a policyholder that a policy has been terminated. The company has the right of cancellation due to non-payment of premiums, or for fraudulent statements made in an application. See also *cancellation provision.*

Numerical Rating System (NRS) a procedure used in life insurance underwriting, in which each factor of physical condition, personal and family history, habits, occupation, hobbies, and demographics is assigned a value. The higher the total count, the greater the risk to the insurance company. A count above a specified level will lead to the conclusion that the risk is substandard, and a policy may be offered at a higher than standard rate. An uninsurable risk is rated at 100. Example: An applicant has a terminal disease, making him an uninsurable risk. The NRS automatically jumps to 100, and the application is rejected. See also *insurable risk; life insurance; risk selection; standard risk; substandard risk; underwriting; uninsurable risk.*

O

occupational accident   an accident that occurs as the direct result of conditions or occurrences in the workplace, or from hazards present. See also *accident and health; disability benefit; workers compensation.*

Occupational Safety and Health Act (OSHA)   a federal law that went into effect in 1971, establishing uniform standards for safety in the workplace. Enforcement was assigned to the U.S. Department of Labor, which was authorized to inspect workplaces, make recommendations for safety improvements, and to report violations. The act also resulted in establishment of the Occupational Safety and Health Administration, which shares the initials of the act itself—OSHA. This is a division of the Department of Labor. See also *disability benefit; workers compensation.*

Occupational Safety and Health Administration (OSHA)   a division of the Department of Labor, created to enforce the provisions of the OSHA law that took effect in 1971. See also *disability benefit.*

occurrence injury theory   the theory that an insurer is liable for claims due to injuries as of the time they occur. In comparison, the manifestation injury theory holds that an insurer is liable only from the time an injury is discovered, or manifests itself. Example: A company carries a liability policy for seven years, and during that time several workers are exposed to hazardous substances. The company later changes insurance companies and, years later, it is discovered that exposed workers have terminal diseases due to the hazard. Under the occurrence injury theory, the insurer that provided coverage during the period of exposure would be liable for claims. See also *liability; long-tail liability; manifestation injury theory.*

occurrence injury theory

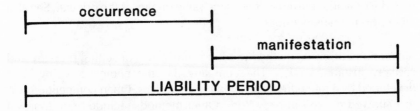

occurrence

manifestation

LIABILITY PERIOD

ocean marine insurance insurance on goods lost or damaged during transport by water. This protection includes losses resulting from collision, sinking or capsizing, fire, piracy, jettison, theft, and other liabilities. Most policies exclude losses due to dampness, decay, mold, wear and tear, and acts of war. See also *casualty insurance; inland marine; marine insurance.*

offer one of the elements necessary in order for a contract to be valid. There must be an offer by one party, and acceptance by the other—a meeting of the minds—before a valid contract can be said to exist. See also *acceptance; contract.*

offset approach a method of funding a retirement plan, in which the maximum benefit to be paid to the participant is reduced by the amount received as Social Security retirement benefits. The same offset provisions may be applied to disability benefits paid under a group plan offered by the employer. See also *disability benefit; retirement plan; Social Security offset.*

Old Age, Survivors, Disability, and Health Insurance (OASDHI) a major segment of the Social Security Act of 1935, providing benefits to workers and their families. It is funded by payroll withholding, and includes the following benefits:
> —old age retirement benefits, paid from the age of 65, with a reduced provision for earlier retirement.
> —payments to disabled workers and their families.
> —payments to surviving spouses of deceased workers, based on the ages of dependent children.

Participation is mandatory for all but public employees, employees of tax-exempt organizations, and certain union employees. The self-employed must pay their own social security benefits by way of the self-employment tax, paid as part of the annual federal income tax return. See also *disability benefit; health insurance; retirement plan; Social Security Act of 1935.*

older homes policy a policy form of homeowner's insurance, designated HO-8. In the event of a loss, the insurance company promises to restore the home to "serviceable" condition. However, there is no guarantee that the material or workmanship will be of the same quality as the original. See also *HO-8; homeowner's insurance.*

open competition a method used in some states for setting property and casualty insurance rates. The company has the choice of using rates developed by a rate bureau, or setting its own rates. Open competition was first allowed in 1969 in New York. Other methods include prior approval rating, a modified version of prior approval, and the file-and-use system. See also *prior approval rating; property and casualty insurance; rate.*

open form   a blanket contract that insures a business against a range of losses that might occur in one or more locations. See also *blanket contract; business liability.*

open policy   a form of marine insurance in which a range of business risks are insured, but the level and time are not specified. Each time a shipment is sent, the insured company submits a listing to the company. The premium is paid based on the level of risk, and not on a pre-established basis. See also *inland marine; marine insurance; ocean marine; property and casualty insurance.*

optional settlement mode   a method under which a beneficiary receives a death benefit. Upon the death of the insured, the beneficiary may receive funds in one of five ways:
   1. Paid in cash.
   2. Left on deposit with the insurance company to accumulate at interest, with earnings to be paid out to the beneficiary periodically.
   3. Payment of a fixed amount. Funds will be paid until the principal amount, plus interest, is exhausted.
   4. Payment for a fixed period. The principal amount, plus interest, is paid out over a calculated period of time, with the amount dependent upon the original sum and the agreed-upon rate of interest to be paid.
   5. Purchase of an annuity, also called the life income option. The death benefit is used as a single annuity premium with proceeds paid for life.
   See also *annuity; beneficiary; death benefit; settlement option.* See illustration, page 148.

ordinary life   one of three broad categories of life insurance business, consisting of term or whole life policies and their variations. The other two categories are group and industrial life.
   Term insurance protects the life of the insured for a specified period of years. A level term policy's face amount does not vary during the term. If the insured desires to renew, the face amount remains the same for the subsequent term, but the amount of premium rises, based on the age of the insured. A decreasing term policy's face amount declines during the term of coverage, but the premium remains the same. At the end of the term, coverage expires.
   Whole life is a combination of insurance and savings. The two, combined, always equal the face amount of the policy, and premiums remain unchanged during the period of insurance. (Some variations of this call for

optional settlement mode

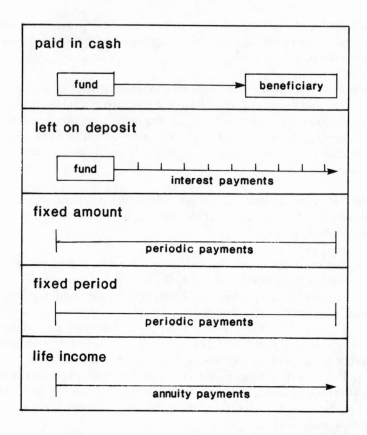

paid in cash

| fund |→| beneficiary |

left on deposit

| fund |→ interest payments

fixed amount

├─ periodic payments ─┤

fixed period

├─ periodic payments ─┤

life income

├─ annuity payments →

---

variable premiums.) As the period of insurance continues, the degree of savings grows and the insurance portion shrinks. This cash value can be borrowed by the policyowner. After a specified number of years, no insurance remains, and the entire policy is represented by cash value. See also *group life; industrial life; life insurance; term life; whole life insurance.*

original age   the age of an insured person as of the effective date of an insurance policy. This age is significant because it is the basis on which the amount of premium is established. In addition, if the policy includes a conversion privilege, an adjustment in rates will be based on the original age. Example: An individual buys a term policy with a conversion period. Three years later, he converts the policy to whole life coverage. The premium is adjusted based on the cost beginning at the original age. See also *attained age; conversion privilege; effective date; term life.*

original cost   the basis in property for the purpose of calculating the amount a company will reimburse following a loss. Property and casualty insurance policies established on the Actual Cash Value (ACV) basis include a provision for depreciation, so that the insured will receive only the depreciated value as of the date of loss. Example: A homeowner's property is destroyed during a fire. Its original cost was $7,200. However, depreciation to date (as calculated by the insurance company) is $4,000. The amount of reimbursement is the net difference, or $3,200. A variation, replacement cost insurance, will reimburse the insured for the amount required to replace lost property at today's cost. However, policies also include limits based on depreciated value. Example: A policy states that it will reimburse covered losses on the replacement cost basis. But the maximum amount is 400% of the depreciated original cost, as would be calculated under an ACV policy. See also *Actual Cash Value (ACV); depreciation; property and casualty insurance; replacement cost.*

over-insurance   the carrying of an excessive amount of insurance coverage, which presents problems both for the insured individual or company, and for the insurance company.

The individual will pay an excessive amount in premium, but can never collect more than the value of lost property (property and casualty insurance). For life insurance protection, it is necessary only to insure against the degree of economic consequence dependents would suffer in the event of premature death.

The insurance company will be concerned when an individual or business carries too much insurance, since that situation could tempt an insured to file exaggerated claims, prolong a hospital stay or disability, or even to falsify the amount of a loss. See also *under-insurance.*

overriding commission   a payment of part of the total commission an agent earns, to a manager. The purpose is to compensate the manager for supervisory and training duties performed at the branch office level. Example: An agent earns a first-year commission of 65% on one type of life insurance policy. By contract, he agrees to an override of 5% of earnings, to be paid to the managing agent. The insurer calculates the override by multiplying the agent's earnings by the override rate. Five percent of 65% is 3.25%. The agent will receive a net commission of 61.75%. Override agreements may vary by line of insurance, or may be established as a portion of the total. Example: If the agreement specifies, the 65% total could be split as 5%

override to the manager, and 60% to the general agent. See also *agent; commission.*

---

overriding commission

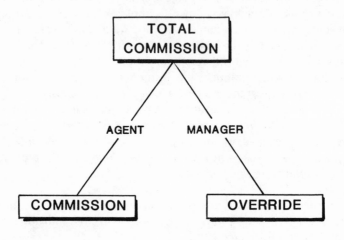

---

owner   the individual who owns a policy of insurance, also called the policyowner. This person is not always the same person as the insured. Example: A father insures the life of his child, is registered as the owner, and pays premiums. Under this form of contract, the owner has the right to request policy loans, convert the policy to a different form of insurance, and select dividend or settlement modes. See also *insured; policyowner.*

ownership rights   the collective rights and privileges held by the owner of an insurance policy. These include the right to:

   —select or change a beneficiary (unless, by agreement, an irrevocable beneficiary has been named or the policy has been assigned);

   —transfer ownership of the policy, through an absolute or a collateral assignment;

   —select a dividend option;

   —select a settlement option in the event of forfeiture;

   —take out cash value by way of a policy loan;

   —exercise conversion rights;

   —terminate the policy.

See also *assignment; cash value; conversion privilege; dividend options; forfeiture; irrevocable beneficiary; policy loan; policyowner; nonforfeiture option; revocable beneficiary; settlement option; termination.*

P

package policy a single policy that covers many losses for a combined periodic premium. This form is common for property and casualty insurance. See also *blanket contract; form; policy; property and casualty insurance; umbrella policy.*

---

package policy

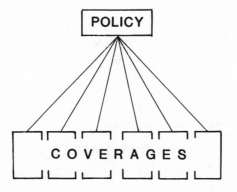

---

paid business descriptive of insurance contracts on which a policy has been issued and the initial premium has been received by the company. See also *earned premium; in force; new business.*

paid-in capital money paid to a company in return for its stock; the ownership portion of a balance sheet that, when added to liabilities, is equal to total admitted assets. See also *capital.*

paid-up addition   one of several dividend options available in participating life insurance policies. The policyowner elects to apply dividends earned to the purchase of paid-up additional life insurance. See also *dividend options; life insurance; participating policy.*

paid-up insurance   a life insurance policy on which all premiums have been paid. This occurs through the payment of a single premium at the beginning of the contract period; or through periodic payments for a specific number of months or years. See also *life insurance; limited payment life; single premium life.*

parent company   the insurer that owns subsidiary companies. Example: A large corporation's stock is listed publicly. However, the company also owns a number of subsidiary companies, in which it is the sole stockholder and parent. See also *insurer.*

---

parent company

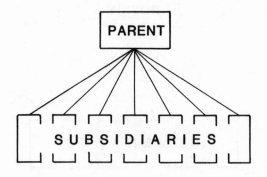

---

partial disability   a disability that, by the definition of a contract, entitles the insured to a portion of benefits only. To receive full benefits, the insured would have to suffer a total disability. Example: A sales executive receives compensation including a base salary and commissions. A broken leg prevents him from field sales activities, although he is still able to perform administrative duties. In this case, the executive has a partial disability. A total disability would prevent the individual from performing all aspects of the job. See also *disability benefit; total disability.*

partial vesting descriptive of the status when an employee is entitled to only a portion of a total retirement fund. Upon full vesting, the entire value belongs to the employee. Example: A retirement plan specifies that each eligible employee must be employed for three years before full vesting. Ownership vests ⅓ each year. The employee leaves after two years, and is 67% vested. See also *full vesting; retirement plan; vesting.*

participating dividend payment to the owner of a participating life insurance policy. The dividend may be received in cash, applied to purchase paid-up additions, applied to future premiums, used to buy term insurance coverage for one year, or left with the insurance company to accumulate at interest. See also *dividend; life insurance.*

participating policy a life insurance policy on which dividends are paid. These dividends are representative of a portion of the company's surplus, and many participating policies guarantee a minimum annual dividend. See also *dividend; life insurance.*

passive retention a form of self-insurance. The individual or company does not provide for contingent losses by purchasing insurance, nor by establishing a reserve. A loss would not be catastrophic and the need for insurance is not great, or a potential loss is not anticipated. See also *retention; self-insurance.*

payment certain a level of payments that is guaranteed under an annuity contract. The company promises to pay out the certain amount, even if the annuitant dies before that benefit is received. In that event, the remainder will be paid to a beneficiary. If the annuitant outlives the certain period, annuity benefits will continue for life or for a specified period of years. See also *annuity; benefit.*

---

payment certain

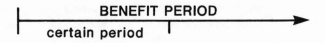

payout phase the period during which the accumulated benefits in an annuity contract are paid out to the annuitant. That period may be for a period certain, for a specified amount of time, or for life. See also *annuity.*

Payroll Stock Ownership Plan (PAYSOP) a form of Employee Stock Ownership Plan (ESOP) popular before passage of the Tax Reform Act of 1986. The PAYSOP gave incentives to employees to participate, by means of a tax credit. This provision was in effect only for the years 1985 and 1986, and was repealed as part of the 1986 act. See also *Employee Stock Ownership Plan (ESOP).*

Pension Benefit Guaranty Corporation (PBGC) an agency established as part of the Employee Retirement Income Security Act of 1974 (ERISA), and part of the Department of Labor. The agency's function is to ensure that participants in defined benefit plans are paid their vested benefits in accordance with the law. See also *Employee Retirement Income Security Act (ERISA); retirement plan.*

pension plan defined benefit or money purchase (defined contribution) plans, in which eligible employees are granted vested interests in retirement benefits. Employers make contributions based on each employee's income, age and years of service. Vesting must occur within a limited number of years. A plan must establish for 100% vesting within five years, or for a minimum of 20% vesting per year beginning at the end of the third year, and 100% by the end of the seventh year. See also *defined benefit plan; money purchase plan; retirement plan.*

per capita "by the person," a method of designating beneficiaries or the division of an estate. Example: The owner of a life insurance policy specifies that four people are to share the proceeds, on a per capita basis. At the time of the owner's death, only three of those people are alive. They will each receive one-third. See also *beneficiary; estate planning.*

per stirpes "by the branch," a method of designating beneficiaries of the division of an estate. Example: The owner of a life insurance policy specifies that four people are to share the proceeds, on a per stirpes basis. At the time of the owner's death, only three of those people are alive. The surviving three each receive one-fourth of the benefits, and the remaining one-fourth is paid to the heirs of the deceased beneficiary. See also *beneficiary; estate planning.*

percentage participating deductible coinsurance in a health insurance policy. The policy states that, after a deductible, it will pay a specified percentage of claims, up to the policy maximum. Example: A policy states that 80% of covered benefits will be paid, while the insured participates—is responsible for—the remaining 20%. See also *coinsurance; health insurance.*

---

percentage
participating deductible

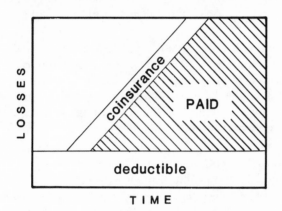

---

peril the loss or situation that could lead to a loss in the future. In property and casualty insurance policies, perils are listed as covered perils or as exclusions, for the purpose of limiting and defining the range of coverage included. See also *loss; property and casualty insurance; risk.*

permanent life whole life insurance; forms of coverage in which cash value accrues over a period of years. The total face amount consists of a combination of insurance and savings. The entire face amount will be paid at any time upon the death of the insured. After a specified period of time has elapsed, the entire face value is made up of savings, and no insurance remains. See also *life insurance; whole life insurance.*

permanent partial disability a partial disability from which no recovery is anticipated. See also *disability benefit; partial disability.*

permanent total disability full disability, defined in most policies as the inability of the insured to perform his or her job, or any job for which that person is reasonably qualified. See also *disability benefit; total disability.*

persistency   the level of insurance policies that stay in force, versus those that lapse. Persistency is a measure of sales and service quality. When the lapse rate is high (thus, persistency is low), it indicates that agents are selling the wrong policies to their market, that they are not servicing their accounts, or that competitors are offering better value for premium dollars. High persistency is a sign of good value and service to the policyowner, on the part of the field and home office force. See also *in force; lapse.*

Personal Automobile Policy (PAP)   a policy that offers casualty and liability protection on automobiles for personal use, as opposed to those used in a business. Sections of the policy include liability, medical payments, uninsured motorist, comprehensive, collision, car rental expense, death or dismemberment, total disability, and loss of earnings. See also *automobile insurance; property and casualty insurance.*

personal contract   a contract concerning the individual, and not that person's property. Life and health insurance policies are examples. Personal contracts cannot be transferred, since the insurance company has agreed to underwrite a specific risk. In addition, upon transfer, the necessary element of insurable interest would be lacking. The rights of personal contracts, in some cases, can be assigned. Example: An individual assigns a lender the beneficiary rights under a life insurance contract until a loan has been repaid in full. See also *contract of insurance; health insurance; life insurance.*

personal history   information about an individual, supplied on an application for insurance, or discovered as part of the underwriting process. The insurance company rates policies based on personal history, including health records, financial status, occupation, hobbies, habits, and family situation. See also *application; insurability; Numerical Rating System (NRS); underwriting.*

personal injury   a form of damage resulting from the acts of an individual. Included are bodily harm, loss of rights, invasion of privacy, slander, libel, false arrest, and defamation of character. See also *liability.*

Personal Producing General Agent (PPGA)   an agent whose sales income is derived from directly written insurance, as well as from overrides from other agents. See also *agent; commission; General Agent (GA); overriding commission.*

personal property   tangible, movable assets, as compared to real estate, which is non-movable. See also *property and casualty insurance; real property.*

policy   a contract of insurance, an agreement between the company and the insured. In return for protection against specified risks, the insured agrees to pay a premium for the term of insurance. See also *contract of insurance; insurer; policyowner.*

policy anniversary   the date 12 months from the effective date of insurance. This anniversary date is significant for a number of reasons:
   1. It is the date from which modal premiums are considered as earned by the insurer.
   2. It is the termination date for term insurance policies.
   3. Establishment of a terminal reserve must be calculated as of the policy anniversary.
   See also *anniversary date.*

policy fee   a one-time fee added to the first premium, to cover the administrative costs of the insurance company during the first year. This cost includes setting up a policy file, issue, underwriting and expense. See also *gross premium; level premium; load; net premium.*

---

policy fee

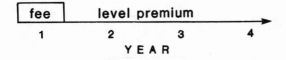

policy loan   an amount borrowed by the policyowner against the cash value of a whole life insurance policy. Any amount up to the surrender value can be borrowed, as a contractual right. The whole life policy consists of a combination of insurance and savings. If the owner dies while a policy loan is outstanding, that amount will be deducted from the total proceeds.
   The policy loan can be requested for any purpose, including payment

of premiums on the policy itself (a premium load). This provision may go into effect immediately upon non-receipt of a due premium, and is called the automatic premium loan. The insurance company has the right to delay granting a requested policy loan for as long as six months, but this provision is rarely enforced. See also *automatic premium loan; cash value; life insurance; surrender value; whole life insurance.*

policyholder the owner or person with rightful possession of a policy, more accurately called the policyowner. A policyholder is often the insured, although not necessarily. Example: A parent buys a contract of insurance on the life of a minor child. In this instance, the parent is the legal policyholder, and the child is the insured. See also *insured.*

policyowner the owner of an insurance contract, including all ownership rights and privileges (to surrender the policy, request a policy loan, and benefits in the event of a loss, specify settlement and dividend options, and exercise conversion rights). See also *insured; ownership rights.*

pool **(1)** a group of insurers who jointly underwrite a class or classes of risks, sharing in the premium income and the payment of claims on an equal or predetermined basis. **(2)** a group of organizations who elect to self-insure against contingent losses. Each contributes a portion of a total reserve. If any losses occur to the members of the group, benefits are paid from the reserve fund. See also *pro rata liability; retention; risk; self-insurance; syndicate.*

---

pool

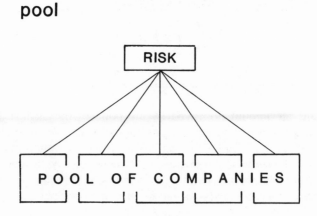

portfolio   the investments held by a person or company. Insurance companies invest funds in a portfolio of stocks, bonds, real estate loans, and other investments. See also *investment income.*

pour-over will   a will specifying that proceeds of the estate are to be transferred to a living trust. See also *estate planning; living trust; trust; will.*

power of attorney   a written authority granted by one person to another, to act in his or her behalf. The document specifies the limits of the power being granted, and for the range of matters and time limits. See also *attorney in fact; principal.*

pre-existing condition   an illness or physical condition that exists before an insurance policy goes into effect. As a rule, health insurance policies exclude pre-existing conditions from coverage. In order for a condition to pre-exist, it must manifest itself. That means the individual knew of the condition due to prior diagnosis, or was aware of the problem at the time a new policy took effect. A life insurance policy granted on the basis of an application is not legal if the insured had a pre-existing condition that was not revealed, and the insurance company discovers it within the first two years of the policy. See also *adverse selection; health insurance; life insurance.*

Preferred Provider Organization (PPO)   a hospital, medical group, physician or specialized medical service that is recommended by an insurance company. By ensuring a volume of business, the insurer is thus able to negotiate lower than average fees for its insured members. See also *health insurance; Health Maintenance Organization (HMO).*

preferred risk   an individual that the insurer considers a lower than standard risk, for the purposes of life or health insurance. Reasons for preferred risks may include profession or lifestyle, for example. See also *insured; risk selection; standard risk.*

preliminary term   a temporary term insurance policy, issued to provide coverage for one year or less. The policy is issued pending replacement with a permanent life insurance policy. See also *life insurance; permanent life; term life.*

premium   the amount an insured pays in exchange for the protection provided by a policy. The total, or gross premium consists of the net premium plus load for commission and administrative expenses. Most forms of insurance contracts include a provision for a level premium payment, either for the entire length of the contract or for a specified term. Others, notably in the health and property and casualty fields, include provisions per periodic experience modification. Premiums generally are assessed on an annual basis, but may also be paid under semiannual, quarterly or monthly modes. See also *experience modification; gross premium; level premium; modal premium; net premium; rate.*

premium deficiency reserve   an additional, temporary reserve for life insurance risks, required by state law when gross premium is below the valuation premium level. See also *deficiency reserve; life insurance; reserve; valuation premium.*

premium discount   a discount allowed for one year's prepayment of an insurance premium. The discount is the estimated present value of the premium as of the future due date. See also *present value; rate.*

premium discount

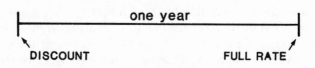

premium load   a loan automatically taken in order to continue payments of premiums that are due on a life insurance policy. Example: A policy has built up cash value, and the policyholder is delinquent on premium payments. Under the contractual premium loan provision, the cash value is reduced by the amount due for current premium. See also *automatic premium loan; cash value; policy loan; whole life insurance.*

premium receipt   a receipt given to the insured as evidence of payment. In the case of a new policy, the initial premium receipt often is given in expectation of approval. Assuming the application is approved, the receipt is binding, and serves as a temporary contract between insurer and insured. If the application is turned down, the initial premium is refunded. See also *binding receipt; initial premium.*

premium tax   a state tax levied against premiums received by insurance companies. This tax is assessed in place of state-level income taxes. See also *state tax.*

present value   the value today of a future sum of money, assuming it will earn a specified rate of return, and that compounding occurs at given intervals. Example: If compounding is done quarterly, the present value of $100 at 8% interest is $92.38. Using a compound interest table for 8% compounded quarterly, the applicable rate is 0.9238454:

$$0.9238454 \times \$100 = \$92.38$$

To prove the result, first divide the interest rate by the number of annual compound periods. In the case of quarterly compounding, divide by 4 (quarters):

$$\frac{.08}{1} = .02$$

Add '1' to this and multiply by the number of periods:

$$1.02 \times 1.02 \times 1.02 \times 1.02 = 1.824321$$

Next, express the factor in decimal form, then multiply by $92.38:

$$1.0824321 \times \$92.38 = \$100.00$$

Stated in another way, the present value of $100, with interest compounded quarterly at 8%, is $92.38.

The above computation is for the "present value of 1," meaning a single sum deposited today will accrue interest by the specified time and at the specified rate, to attain the desired fund.

To calculate the amount required to accumulate a desired fund, when a series of deposits will be made, it is necessary to refer to the compound interest table called "sinking fund factors." Example: You need to determine how much money must be deposited today to accumulate $5,000 in three years, assuming semiannual compounding at 9%.

Looking at the semiannual compound interest table for sinking fund factors, the correct factor is 0.1488784. To accumulate $5,000, it will be necessary to make a series of deposits:

$$0.1488784 \times \$5,000 = \$744.39$$

To prove that this is accurate, calculate the amount of interest accumulated on each of six semiannual deposits. The following assumes interest is payable at the *end* of each period. Because interest is compounded semiannually, the annual rate of 9% is halved to 4.5%. (Note: Interest for each period is calculated in the previous period's ending balance.)

Period	Deposit	Interest	Balance
1	$744.39	$ –	$ 744.39
2	744.39	33.50	1,522.28
3	744.39	68.50	2,335.17
4	744.39	105.08	3,184.64
5	744.39	143.31	4,072,34
6	744.39	183.26	4,999.99

See also *accumulated value; compound interest; sinking fund; time value of money.* See illustrations below and on page 163.

present value (of 1)

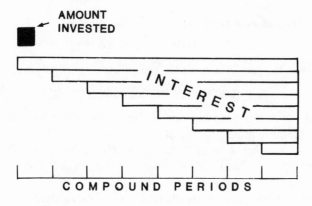

AMOUNT INVESTED

INTEREST

COMPOUND PERIODS

presumptive disability the belief that a disability is total, due to the nature of an injury. Example: An insured person loses both legs in an accident. It is presumed that disability is total and permanent. However, the individual does eventually begin earning a living once again. Benefits under a disability income policy will be paid in accordance with policy terms. The benefit may be paid as a lump sum at the time the presumptive disability occurs, representing the maximum benefit allowable; or continuing payments may cease upon the return to work. See also *disability income; total disability.*

primacy guidelines concerning the order and amount of payment, when more than one policy covers a single loss. An insured person cannot recover

present value (of a series of deposits)

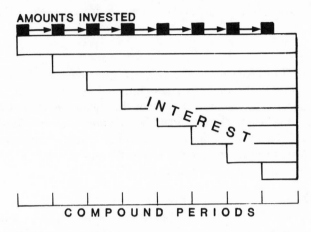

an amount in excess of the loss, so primacy is applied to multiple policies, based on coverage terms, dates policies were entered, and other factors. See also *Coordination of Benefits (COB); over-insurance.*

primary beneficiary   the individual named in a life insurance policy who will receive benefits in the event of death. If the insured outlives the primary beneficiary, a named contingent beneficiary will be paid. See also *beneficiary; contingent beneficiary; life insurance.*

Primary Insurance Amount (PIA)   the maximum amount of insurance a company will pay in the event of a loss, considering deductible, coinsurance, and the possibility of duplicate coverage via other policies. See also *benefit; coinsurance; Coordination of Benefits (COB); deductible; over-insurance.*

principal   (1) the applicant for insurance, later to become the policyowner or the insured. (2) the grantor of representation rights in a principal and agency relationship. See also *agent; insured.*

prior approval rating   one method of rate rules, used in some states. Before offering property and casualty policies to the public, the insurance company must obtain prior approval from the state. Alternative plans, used in certain states, include the modified prior approval and the open competition methods. See also *open competition; property and casualty insurance; rate.*

pro rata distribution   a blanket contract, one that provides business liability coverage when covered property is kept in several locations. See also *blanket contract; business liability; open form; property and casualty insurance.*

pro rata liability   coinsurance among two or more companies, covering the same property. Example: A large company purchases a property and casualty policy on its inventory. However, the maximum possible loss is too great for the one insurer to carry. So the loss is coinsured with a pool of other companies. Each carries a pro rata share of premium income and, in the event of a loss, also carries a pro rata share of the total. See also *coinsurance; pool; property and casualty insurance.*

probability   the chance that an event will occur at some time in the future. Depending on the type of insurance, probability calculations will vary. Example: for life insurance, death is a certainty. However, the time of death cannot be known. In this case, probability is calculated based on the average number of deaths that will occur, on average, for each age group. In liability insurance, a specific loss might or might not occur. However, the insurer knows that, on average, an approximate number of losses will occur within a large group of risks. Thus, all of the insured in that group can be assessed a premium adequate to pay the estimated number of losses.

Calculating probability is based on identifying known likely events. Example: A coin flip has a 50% chance of coming up heads, and a 50% chance of coming up tails. However, the probability is more complex when two coin flips are considered:

description	probability
heads, heads	25%
heads, tails	25%
tails, heads	25%
tails, tails	25%

Note that both the outcome and the timing are broken out in this example. Timing is an important element of insurance probability, since an estimate of the occurrence of a probable risk affects premium and reserve requirements, equally as much as the cost of a loss.

To expand, a series of three coin flips could come up in one of two ways: There is a 25% probability that it will result in all heads, or in all tails; and a 75% chance of a 2 to 1 mix. But when the timing of these possible events is studied, the probability is more diverse:

description	probability
heads, heads, heads	12.5%
heads, heads, tails	12.5%
heads, tails, tails	12.5%
heads, tails, heads	12.5%
tails, tails, tails	12.5%
tails, tails, heads	12.5%
tails, heads, heads	12.5%
tails, heads, tails	12.5%

The coin flip is greatly simplified, since there are only two possible outcomes in a single toss. However, it makes the point: An actuary knows that, on average, one of the events above will occur one time in every eight. If it was necessary to insure against any one of those outcomes, it would be possible to calculate losses and frequency of occurrence, then to arrive at a required premium to charge. See also *actuary; law of large numbers.*

probability distribution the likelihood that a specific event will occur. Actuaries depend on the law of large numbers in assessing risks. Example: A mortality table indicates that of all males of a specific age, so many will die each year. On the basis of population-based averages, these estimates are very accurate. However, if only a few lives are studied, actual experience will vary from the probability distribution. See also *law of large numbers.*

probate the legal settlement of an estate in which the will is validated, the property of the deceased is distributed, and the heirs receive their rightful share of assets. See also *estate planning; heir; will.*

probate estate that portion of a deceased's estate that is subject to the jurisdiction of the probate court. Not all assets of an estate are transferred by will. Example: The beneficiary of a life insurance policy is granted benefits by contract, and not by will. See also *estate planning; joint tenants; will.*

probationary period also called the elimination period, the number of days from the effective date of a policy during which an insured cannot receive benefits. This comes about from a contractual agreement. The contract in a group health policy may state that new employees cannot be covered under a policy until a probationary period has passed. The probationary period should not be confused with the elimination period common in disability income policies, stating that benefits will not begin until a number of days has elapsed from the day disability begins. See also *elimination period; health insurance.*

proceeds   the benefit or settlement amount paid from the insurer to the insured or a beneficiary, under a contract of insurance. See also *benefit; settlement.*

producer   an agent or broker; the term is used in the insurance business to describe one who sells insurance to the public, and earns a commission. See also *agent; broker.*

production   the amount of new business generated by an agent or broker. In life insurance, production is represented by the face amount of policies in force. In health and property or liability insurance, it is the total amount of written premium. See also *face amount; in force; new business; premium; written premium.*

professional liability insurance   insurance that is intended specifically for the risks to which professionals are exposed. Example: Attorneys, physicians, dentists and accountants stand a high risk of malpractice liability. See also *business liability; liability insurance; malpractice liability.*

profit sharing plan   a form of qualified retirement plan in which the employer sets aside a portion of annual profits. This fund accrues to the vested benefits of eligible employees, to be paid upon retirement, death, disability or termination of employment.
  The profit sharing plan is advantageous to the employer. In years of low profits or even losses, the business is not required to contribute to the plan. In comparison, a pension plan, where contributions are to be made based on salaries, a cash flow hardship can be created in certain years. See also *qualified plan; retirement plan.*

prohibited risk   any risk that the insurer will not select. Example: A life insurance company will not provide insurance to any individual who has been diagnosed with a potentially fatal disease. Such an individual is an uninsurable risk. See also *adverse selection; risk selection; uninsurable risk.*

proof of loss   a form of document or other proof that is acceptable to the insurer in the event of a casualty or other loss, as specified by the contract. Example: A life insurance contract defines a death certificate as acceptable proof of loss. And under the terms of an automobile policy, the insured is required to present the automobile to a company adjuster, so that the extent of loss can be determined. See also *loss.*

property and casualty insurance   policies that protect individuals and businesses against the economic losses resulting from casualties and liabilities related to their property.

An example of a casualty: A loss from a covered peril, such as the loss of business inventory due to theft; or the total loss of a home covered under a homeowner's policy, due to a fire.

An example of a liability: Damage done to a neighbor's property due to conditions on the insured's property (a limb falling from a tree and damaging another home's roof); or injury to another person while on the insured's property.

The liability policy includes several standard provisions, including:

perils—the specific limitations, inclusions and exclusions covered by the policy.

requirements—specific rules for written notification of loss, evidence of loss, loss prevention practices the insured is required to place and keep in force, submission of a loss inventory, and the agreement to submit to a site examination.

other insurance—a clause stating how Coordination of Benefits (COB) will be applied, in the event of double coverage of insured losses.

subrogation—the right retained by the insurer to seek reimbursement for losses to covered property that are caused by another.

cancellation—conditions under which the policy may be cancelled.

See also *cancellation provision; Coordination of Benefits (COB); evidence clause; loss prevention; peril; subrogation.*

proportional reinsurance an arrangement of coinsurance among two or more insurers. Under this arrangement, all premium income and loss expenses are shared on the same percentage basis. See also *coinsurance; reinsurance.*

prospect an individual considered by an agent to be a potential buyer of insurance. To qualify, the person must be:

  —willing to purchase insurance
  —need insurance protection
  —able to afford premium payments
  —an insurable risk

See also *application; insurable risk; underwriting.*

prospective reserve the amount of reserve required to pay future claims. At the time the policy is initiated, the estimated present value of future premiums is equal to the estimated present value of future benefits. As each premium payment is made, this relationship changes. Thus, a reserve must be established and adjusted to maintain the balance of future values. See also *Net Level Premium (NLP); present value; reserve; Retrospective Method (RM); terminal reserve.*

protection and indemnity insurance an expanded form of marine insurance. This coverage expands to losses due to actions of a crew during transport; damages to other objects; and several other provisions not found in the standard policy. See also *liability insurance; marine insurance.*

prudent man rule a concept that is meant to guide the actions of agents and fiduciaries. It states that no actions should be taken in behalf of another person that would not be taken by a reasonably prudent man. Example: A trustee may place money in the trust in an investment other than a list of approved investments, as long as the trustee is acting under the prudent man rule. However, the trustee, by terms of the agreement, is limited in the portion of the trust assets that can be invested apart from the restrictive list. See also *agent; fiduciary; investment income.*

public liability in general, all insurance coverages for property damages, physical injuries to others, and related risks. See also *blanket contract; Comprehensive General Liability (CGL); liability; package policy; scheduled policy.*

pure annuity an annuity in which the annuitant receives payments for the remainder of his or her life. This benefit continues regardless of the number of years the annuitant survives; thus, no provisions are made for payments to survivors or beneficiaries. See also *annuity; refund annuity.*

pure annuity

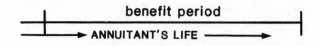

pure endowment a rare form of endowment in which payment is made to the insured only if he or she is living at the end of a specified period of years. If the insured dies during that period, no benefit is paid. See also *endowment; life insurance.*

Pure Premium Rating Method (PPRM) a calculation of the actual future cost of claims based on net premiums (before loading is added). It is calculated by dividing expected losses by the number of exposures. Example:

An insurer estimates the cost of residential fire losses over the next 10 years at $16 million. The number of policyholders is estimated during the same period at 7,000. Under the PPRM calculation, the pure premium cost to the company is $2,285.71 per policy over the 10-year period. Net premium for each of the 10 years will be calculated based on the present value of that total, given an assumed rate of interest. See also *loss; rate; risk.*

Pure Premium Rating Method (PPRM)

$$\frac{\text{expected losses}}{\text{exposure}}$$

---

pure risk   descriptive of a risk in which a loss will either occur, or will not occur. Example: A homeowner purchases a fire insurance policy. In recent years, 1.6% of all residences had losses of one type or another. Thus, on average, there is a small chance of a loss and a larger chance of no loss. Without considering the probability, the only certainty is that one of two outcomes will take place. A life insurance policy involves a different form of risk. Everyone who keeps a policy in force will eventually die, as a certainty. The risk is that no one knows when a specific death will occur. See also *probability; risk; standard risk.*

pyramiding   the practice of purchasing two or more policies to insure against the same risks. This could lead to the temptation to overstate or falsify claims. Thus, through the industry practice known as Coordination of Benefits (COB), an insured cannot receive more than the total amount of a loss. See also *Coordination of Benefits (COB); over-insurance.*

Q

qualified impairment   a type of coverage for which the insurance company will pay only a limited benefit in the event of loss. Example: An individual has a past history of kidney problems. Upon offering a contract of insurance, the company identifies this as a qualified impairment, and places a dollar limit on the amount it will pay in related losses. See also *health insurance; special risk; substandard risk.*

qualified plan   a form of retirement plan that has qualified for deductibility of contributions and for tax deferral of benefits. Requirements include a fixed formula for contributions, based either on the employer's profits, or on the basis of salary, age and years of service. In addition, vesting must accrue to 100% within a limited number of years, and employees must be able to receive benefits starting at an identified retirement age. See also *Individual Retirement Account (IRA); Keogh plan; pension plan; profit sharing plan; retirement plan.*

quota share reinsurance   a form of automatic reinsurance, in which a prescribed portion of all income is paid from the direct writer to the reinsurer; and the same portion of losses are absorbed by the reinsurance company. The quota share applies to all insurance written within a specified category of business. See also *reinsurance; retention.*

---

quota share reinsurance

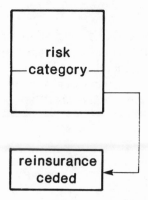

R

rate   the amount charged per unit of insurance. In life insurance, rates are set per $1,000 of insurance, based on the age and sex of the applicant. Disability income rates are based on the amount of monthly benefit at a given age. Rates are developed based on actuarial estimates of future losses, and a factor is added for commissions, the cost of administration, state premium taxes, and profit margin. The result is the gross unit cost. Premium is the number of units purchased, times the gross rate. See also *policy fee; premium; standard risk.*

rate discrimination   the practice of charging different rates to classes of applicants, based on geographic, racial, economic or other premises. The practice is illegal. See also *discrimination; redlining; risk selection.*

rate making   the setting of rates for insurance coverages. The rate cannot discriminate as defined by state law; it must be adequate to pay for future losses through the establishment of a reserve; and it must be competitive with the rates charged by other insurers for similar lines of coverage. The net premium is calculated based on expected losses or, for certain types of insurance, based on experienced losses. To this is added a loading factor for commissions, premium taxes, contingencies, administrative expenses, and a margin of profit. The resulting rate, multiplied by the units purchased, is the gross premium charged. See also *discrimination; gross premium; net premium; reserve.*

rate of disability   the probable number of claims that are expected to occur during a specified period of time, or at a specified age. The insurer must estimate the rate in order to establish its own risk exposure and establish reserves and premium levels. See also *disability benefit; probability; risk.*

rate of return   **(1)** a factor reported by insurers, of the percentage it collected in premium dollars that is returned in the form of benefits. Example: A health insurer advises its policyholders that it has returned 97% of premiums in the form of claims. **(2)** a calculation of investment income earned, expressed as a percentage. For example, an individual invests $30,000 and, seven months later, sells the investment for $32,850. The profit of $2,850, when divided by the amount invested, is a return of 9.5%. For purposes of comparison, the rate of return should be expressed in annualized form. Since the holding period in this example was seven months, the rate of return should be divided by 7 (months) and multiplied by 12 (months), to arrive at the annualized return of 16.3%.

In cases where an investment is held longer than one year, the average annualized rate is calculated in the same way. If an investment yielded 35.5% and was held for 27 months, the average annual return would be 15.8% (35.5% divided by 27; the result multiplied by 12). However, an exact calculation of long-term return must also be calculated assuming different time values of money over the holding period. For example, an investor averages a 15.8% return over 27 months. The time value of that return is greater during the earlier years, assuming that money could have been invested for compound interest, over a longer period of time. Later yields are worth relatively less, because the levels of time and opportunity are shorter. See also *compound interest; investment income; time value of money; Yield To Maturity (YTM)*.

rate of return

$$\frac{\text{current value} - \text{original cost}}{\text{original cost}} = \text{total return}$$

$$\frac{\text{total return}}{\text{holding period}} \times 1 \text{ year} = \text{annual return}$$

$$\frac{\$32,850 - \$30,000}{\$30,000} = 9.5\%$$

$$\frac{9.5\%}{7} \times 12 = 16.3\%$$

Rate of Return Method (RRM) **(1)** a method for calculating the rate of return earned by the owner of a whole life insurance policy, on the savings portion of that policy.

The gross premium is reduced by the amount of the pure cost of insurance (the premium required to establish a reserve for future claims), and by any dividends paid, if applicable. The remainder is then compared to the final cash value of the policy. The rate of return is the compound rate required, given the amount of available premium, to create that level of savings.

(2) a procedure for calculating the economic value of an individual's current earnings, given the assumed number of future years and earnings levels he or she is likely to realize. The likely rate is then compared to the economic consequences to a family, business partners, or others with an insurable interest, if that person is disabled or dies. The purpose of the computation is to estimate the value and need for insurance coverage. See also *cash value; dividend; economic value; expected mortality; gross premium; Interest Adjusted Cost (IAC); life insurance; needs approach; whole life insurance.*

rated policy   a policy issued on a risk that, in the opinion of the underwriter, is greater than the average risk. As a consequence, the company will agree to provide insurance only with a higher than standard premium; with reduced or limited levels of coverage; or excluding certain, specified perils. See also *premium; risk; substandard risk; underwriting.*

real property   land, structures and other permanent additions to land, excluding personal property. For the purpose of defining the scope of coverage in a property and casualty insurance policy, real and personal property are distinguished under this definition. See also *personal property; property and casualty insurance.*

rebate   **(1)** a dividend paid to a policyholder, representing a partial reimbursement of premium. **(2)** a reduction in insurance rates, based on favorable experience. **(3)** payment to the insured of part of an agent's commission, as an incentive to buy insurance, a practice that is illegal. See also *commission; dividend; retroactive rate reduction.*

recurring disability clause   a clause in a health insurance policy defining the conditions under which disability benefits will continue to be paid. When an insured is disabled and then returns to work, a relapse will be considered a new claim. However, the policy may state that, if the relapse occurs within a limited amount of time, it will be treated as a continuation of the same disability. In that case, a deductible will not be applied against benefits. See also *deductible; disability benefit; health insurance.*

redlining   the illegal practice of failing or refusing to underwrite risks in an area, or based on racial or economic factors. See also *discrimination; rate discrimination; underwriting.*

reduced paid-up insurance   insurance provided as a nonforfeiture option. A life insurance policy accumulates cash value over time, and may be paid to the insured in one of several ways. If the insured chooses, paid-up additions can be purchased with proceeds. The cash value is then used as premiums on additional permanent insurance of a lower amount. See also *cash value; life insurance; nonforfeiture option; paid-up addition.*

---

reduced paid-up insurance

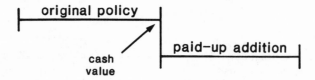

---

reentry term life   a form of Yearly Renewable Term (YRT) insurance allowing the insured to apply for continued coverage at the expiration of specified terms (usually in five-year increments). The benefit of this provision is that continued insurance will be provided at a lower rate than would apply for new policies, given the insured's attained age. However, the policy might also state that, in order to qualify, the insured must submit evidence of insurability. See also *attained age; evidence of insurability; life insurance; renewable term life; term life; Yearly Renewable Term (YRT).*

---

reentry term life

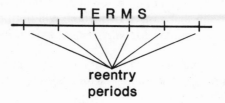

refund annuity   a form of annuity that guarantees to refund the full cost of purchase, even if the annuitant dies before that level has been reached. In that event, the balance of payments will be made to the named beneficiary. If the insured outlives the refund period, payments will continue for life, or for the maximum guaranteed annuity period. See also *annuity; certain payment; pure annuity.*

---

refund annuity

annuitization

life

refund period

---

regional office   the agency office or branch office of an insurance company. This term may be applied to a fully owned office, or to an office owned and operated by an independent agency. The regional office usually limits its activity to selling and servicing insurance accounts. However, in certain larger companies, regional offices also provide marketing, administrative and underwriting services to its agency force. See also *agency; broker-agent; captive agent; independent agent.*

reinstatement   the reversal of a lapsed policy, within a period of time specified by contract. The insurance company has the right to require evidence of insurability, on the basis of additional risk when a policy has lapsed. The principle of adverse selection (that an individual who is aware of a condition is more likely to want insurance, than one who is not aware) increases the risks to the insurance company.

Reinstatement can be advantageous to an individual based on current age. Even though unpaid premiums, plus interest and any outstanding policy loans must be repaid to the company, the cost of a new policy would be higher, because the attained age is greater now than at the time the policy originally was contracted. See also *adverse selection; attained age; evidence of insurability; lapse.*

reinsurance   the practice of sharing risks with other insurers. Example: One company establishes its retention limit at $20,000. This means it will not assume the risk on any one policy that exceeds that level. An individual applies for a policy for $100,000 of life insurance. The company approves the policy, but cedes $80,000 to a reinsurance company. All premiums received are split on a 20/80 basis with the reinsurance company, and all claims are also to be paid on the same basis. See also *proportional reinsurance; retention.*

---

reinsurance

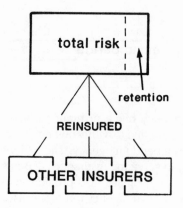

---

reinsurance assumed insurance business on the books of a company that has accepted risks from another company. The assumed portion relates to income, reserves, and claims actually paid. See also *retention; risk.*

reinsurance capacity the greatest level or retention limit a company will allow on a single risk. Example: The retention capacity of one company is $20,000 on any one life. When a $100,000 policy is sold, $80,000 is ceded to a second company. However, that company has its own capacity limit of $30,000. It, in turn, may cede the excess of $50,000 to another company. It is more likely, however, that a pool of companies will establish a reinsurance treaty, agreeing to underwrite portions of each risk that exceeds retention levels. See also *pool; retention; risk.* See illustration, page 177.

reinsurance capacity

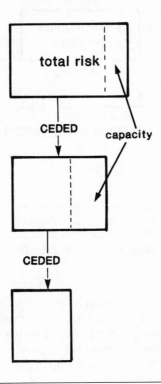

---

reinsurance ceded   insurance that is assigned to another company. On the writing company's books, this appears as a reduction of premium, reserves, and claims. See also *retention; risk.*

reinsurance treaty   an agreement entered by two or more insurance companies, to share certain risks in a defined line of business. Example: Three companies agree to share insurance above retention levels on the basis of 50-20-30%. Each of the companies will receive that percentage of income, establish the appropriate reserve, and pay the proportionate amount of all future claims. See also *retention; risk.* See illustration, page 178.

remainder   **(1)** in reinsurance, the amount of risk left after the writing company deducts its own retention limits; the portion that must be reinsured. **(2)**

reinsurance treaty

---

that portion of an estate left over after specified gifts and bequests have been made. See also *estate planning; residue; retention; risk.*

renewable term life   a form of term life insurance allowing the insured to continue coverage for added terms, up to a limit established by the contract. This option is exercised without the insured having to provide evidence of insurability, as long as the policy is kept in force. However, the amount of premium to be paid is raised with each term, based on the insured's attained age. See also *attained age; evidence of insurability; life insurance; reentry term life; term life.*

---

renewable term life

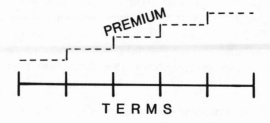

renewal clause   (1) the clause in an insurance contract specifying the right to continue coverage after the expiration of a term. The amount of insurance remains the same, and the premium is increased based on the age of the insured. (2) terms and conditions for reinstatement of a lapsed policy. Specified in the clause are time limits for applying, the requirement for evidence of insurability, and the immediate payment of back premiums plus interest. See also *in force; reinstatement.*

renewal premium   (1) the premium charged after the first full year of coverage. In certain types of policies, the premium may be increased or decreased, depending on actual loss experience. This experience modification enables the insurer to maintain its loss reserves at a reasonable level, and to better manage risks by segmentation.
   (2) for the purposes of computing commissions to be paid to agents, renewal premium is subject to a substantially lower rate than first-year premium. See also *commission; experience modification; premium; replacement.*

renewal term   any form of term life insurance in which the policyowner has the right to renew at the end of the term, without evidence of insurability. The contract sets a limit on the maximum age, beyond which it will not allow renewal. And premium costs increase with each renewal, based on the insured's attained age. See also *attained age; evidence of insurability; life insurance; term life.*

renter's policy   a form of homeowner's insurance, also called HO-4, designed especially for renters. Because the structure the renter occupies is owned by someone else (and, it must be assumed, is insured separately), insurance coverage under the renter's policy is limited only to perils to personal property. See also *HO-4; homeowner's insurance; property and casualty insurance.*

replacement   the cancellation of one insurance policy and substitution of another. Agents from one company may attempt to convince an individual that their product is a better value for the same money, that premiums are lower, or that service is superior. Agents who previously sold a policy might attempt to replace one policy with another to create a new first-year premium, for which the commission will be substantially higher than that paid on renewals. See also *Lapse Ratio (LR); policy; twisting.*

replacement cost   one of two forms of property and casualty insurance. In this form, the insured will receive an amount of money required to replace lost property, regardless of its age. The alternative is Actual Cash Value

(ACV insured, under which only the depreciated value of property can be recovered. While replacement cost coverage yields a higher portion of losses, it is also limited. Example: One policy specifies that replacement cost will be limited to no more than 400% of the ACV-computed value (after depreciation). A policyholder reports the theft of a stereo system that originally cost $1,100, and would cost $1,350 to replace today. The ACV basis of this property is only $200. So regardless of actual replacement cost, the maximum the policyholder can receive is $800: 400% of the $200 ACV value. See also *Actual Cash Value (ACV); casualty insurance; depreciation; property and casualty insurance.*

replacement ratio   a ratio showing the level of lapses experienced by an individual insurance agent. The purpose is to judge the agent's performance in terms of ability to sell insurance that remains in force; selecting the best possible candidates for the products sold; service provided after the sale; and competitive value with other agents. The ratio can be computed on the basis of the number of policies, the amount of premium, or—most often—on the amount of new business in force and replaced. Example: One agent places $835,000 of new business during a one-year period. Of that total, $300,000 is replaced during the year. On the basis of the amount in force, 35.9% was replaced. See also *face amount; Lapse Ratio (LR); life insurance; new business; twisting.*

---

replacement ratio

$$\frac{\text{replaced face amount}}{\text{total new business}}$$

$$\frac{\$300,000}{\$835,000} = 35.9\%$$

---

rescission   **(1)** the right under the federal Truth in Lending Act, of a party to a contract to cancel the agreement within three days from the date of signing. Upon rescission, all money paid to the other side must be reimbursed without penalty.

(2) the act of cancellation of a contract based on discovered fraud or misrepresentation. Such acts make contracts void. Example: An insurer discovers during the first two years a policy is in force that the insured included false statements at the time the application was completed. The company cancels the contract.

(3) a legal procedure undertaken to cancel the provisions of any contract. See also *contract; fraudulent misrepresentation; void contract.*

reserve   a liability established for the purpose of paying future claims. The present value of the amount established as a reserve is estimated to be equal to the present value of all future claims. See also *active life reserves; actuarial present value; legal reserve; present value; probability.*

reserve value   the current value accumulated under a policy, representing the computed present value of future claims that may arise as provided in that policy. See also *life insurance; present value.*

resident agent   an insurance agent living in the state in which insurance products are sold. See also *agent; licensed agent.*

residual disability   as defined in a disability income policy, a partial disability. Benefits will be paid according to the degree of inability to work. For example, an insured is totally disabled for several months, and begins to recover. During the recovery period, that individual is able to work for 10 hours per week. The difference between a full week's earnings and the amount earned in 10 hours is residual. Benefits will be scaled down accordingly. See also *disability income.*

residue   the remainder, the balance left in an estate after payment of specified bequests. See also *estate planning; remainder.*

retained earnings   that portion of a business' net worth accumulated through net profits not paid out in the form of dividends. Example: A company earns $4,800,000 in a one-year period, after all expenses. It declares a $200,000 total dividend for participating policyholders, and a $1,000,000 dividend to be paid to stockholders. The balance, $3,600,000, is added to retained earnings. See also *net worth.*

retention   the highest amount of risk an insurance company will carry on any one case. For example, one company sets its retention at $20,000. All approved policies above that level will be partly reinsured, with the writing company keeping only the first $20,000 of risk (and corresponding premiums, reserves and exposure to claims). See also *reinsurance; risk.*

retirement age   the age at which an employee may begin to receive full benefits under the terms of a pension, profit sharing or other retirement plan. If the employee wants benefits before that date, the total amount received is either reduced or (under the rules for IRA's and Keogh plans) is subject to tax penalties. See also *Individual Retirement Account (IRA); Keogh plan; normal retirement age; pension plan; profit sharing plan.*

retirement income policy   a form of annuity created as part of a life insurance policy. During the insurance period, premiums are paid for protection against the economic consequences of early death. Upon retirement, installment payments are made by the company and will continue for life or for a specified number of months. Electing to receive a monthly income rather than a lump sum is one form of settlement option under a life insurance policy. In this instance, an annuity is created, with the full cash value used as a single premium on the annuity contract. See also *annuity; deferred annuity; life insurance; settlement option.*

retirement income policy

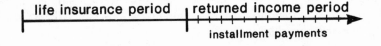

retirement plan   (1) part of a financial plan, in which investments, insurance and assets are valued and planned over many years. Ultimately, the purpose is to minimize expenses and provide insurance during retirement. Insurance also protects the individual against the economic consequences of unexpected losses.

(2) any form of insurance product designed to provide income during retirement.

(3) one of several plans offered by an employer, entered into by an individual, or established for the purpose of providing financial security and income during retirement years. See also *deferred annuity; financial plan;*

Individual Retirement Account (IRA); Keogh plan; pension plan; profit sharing plan; qualified plan.

retroactive rate reduction   an experience refund or reduction of subsequent year's premium based on favorable loss experience. See also *experience refund.*

Retrospective Method (RM)   a method of calculating reserves. An initial assumption is made regarding the required terminal reserve. This is then modified periodically, based on actual losses experienced. See also *benefit; reserve; terminal reserve.*

retrospective rating   an experience modification, or adjustment of rates charged based on actual losses in comparison to estimated losses. Example: Losses last year were 97% of the expected loss levels. The initial annual premium charged to one company was $1,863. The following year, the rate is reduced by $56:

$$\$1,863 \times 97\% = \$1,807$$

Example: Losses exceeded expected levels for one policy by five percent. The subsequent year's premium is thus modified to reflect the higher than expected losses, by $93:

$$\$1,863 \times 105\% = \$1,956$$

See also *experience modification; premium.*

return commission   the amount paid to an agent for selling a policy, that must be returned to the company because the policy lapses or is cancelled by the insured. See also *commission; lapse.*

return of premium   **(1)** a rider occasionally added to the provisions of a life insurance policy, stating that in the event of death within a certain period of time, the insured will receive the full face amount, plus a return of all premiums paid until that point.

(2) a provision in some health insurance policies, that the policyholders will be paid a benefit for the total amount of premiums paid until that point, minus claims paid.

(3) a provision in a disability income policy intended to discourage filing of claims for limited disabilities. It states that of total premiums paid over a period of time (often 10 years), a percentage will be refunded to the policyholder if no claims have been submitted; or that percentage, minus any claims, will be paid. See also *disability income; health insurance; premium.*

Reverse Annuity Mortgage (RAM)   a program that combines a home mortgage with an annuity. A policyholder, in order to qualify, must be of a certain age (usually 62). The program is designed for retired people with limited income and high equity in their homes. The insurer pays a monthly benefit, which accrues at interest and creates a mortgage. The annuitant must reimburse the insurer at some future date, either an identified time in the future or upon death. The equity in the home will be used to reimburse the advance annuity payments.

   Risk to the insurance company in a life annuity is that the individual will outlive the equity level. Thus, payments will be greater than the amount the insurer could recover through an eventual sale. For this reason, many RAM programs identify a future date after which the house must be sold, and the mortgage side of the annuity settled. See also *annuity; equity.*

Reverse Annuity Mortgage (RAM)

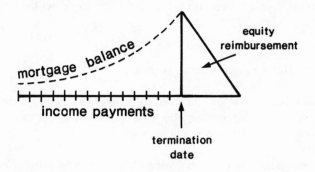

reversionary interest   (1) the interest held by the beneficiary in joint life and survivors annuities. Under terms of this policy, payments continue for as long as the latest surviving spouse continues to live.

   (2) the interest held by an individual, in the future use and value of property presently held by another person. See also *annuity; beneficiary; joint life and survivors annuity; survivorship annuity.* See illustration, page 185.

reversionary trust   a form of trust in which the property in question will be returned to the grantor at some future date. During the time the trust is

reversionary interest

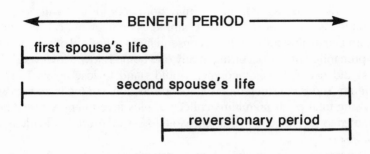

in effect, the trust recipient earns income earned on the property. See also *trust.*

revocable beneficiary   a beneficiary that can be removed at the option of the policyowner. Under revocable terms, the policyowner also has the right to assign cash value or to take out a policy loan. See also *beneficiary; irrevocable beneficiary.*

revocable trust   a form of trust that, at the grantor's option, can be revoked and cancelled. See also *irrevocable trust; trust.*

rider   an endorsement, or additional provisions, added to an insurance contract to provide additional protection, increased coverage limits, or special conditions. Typical riders include:

accidental death — extra benefits will be paid in the event that death occurs as the result of an accident.

additional insurance — extra amounts of insurance are added, in return for which an additional premium is paid.

Cost of Living Adjustment (COLA) — coverage limits are raised in accordance with changes in the cost of living.

guaranteed insurability — this rider gives the insured a guarantee that insurance coverage will be continued for additional terms, and that the insurance company cannot cancel the policy.

Waiver of Premium (WP) — a rider that keeps insurance in force without premiums being paid, when the insured is disabled and unable to make payments.

See also *accidental death; additional insured contract; Cost of Living*

Adjustment (COLA); endorsement; guaranteed insurability; policy; Waiver of Premium (WP).

risk exposure to loss that may or may not occur; or that will occur, but when the insured does not know. Example: A homeowner carries a policy that protects against the economic consequences of fire and other casualties. The probability of this occurring in any one home is low. However, if such a loss did occur, the homeowner would stand to lose a lot. Thus, the premium paid is considered reasonable protection. For the insurance company, the total of all premiums collected, plus investment net income, is estimated to be adequate for all probable losses to insured individuals and businesses.

Life insurance is a different form of protection. Death is a certainty, but its timing cannot be known in advance. Thus, life policies protect the beneficiary against the economic losses that would result if death occurred prematurely. See also *insurability; probability; pure risk; standard risk; substandard risk.*

Risk and Insurance Management Society (RIMS) an association of individuals, professionals and business executives whose functions include the purchase of insurance protection, or structuring of self-insurance programs. See also *insured; risk management.*

risk classification a division of risks used by underwriters to identify the probability and degree of loss in specific classes. The result of a classification study is clarification of rates necessary to protect the insurance company against excessive future losses, and to ensure that premium levels are adequate for those claims. See also *policy; standard risk; substandard risk; underwriting.*

risk management descriptive of practices to reduce risk and the possibility of loss; or to ensure that adequate insurance coverage is carried in the event that losses do occur. Procedures include the identification of contingencies and sources of loss; estimates of risk exposure and the financial consequences those risks carry; and methods to reduce the likelihood of future losses, such as safety programs in the workplace. See also *catastrophic loss; estate planning; loss; loss prevention; passive retention; self-insurance.*

risk selection the method by which underwriters decide whether or not to offer a contract of insurance. The underwriter must be concerned with several issues, including:

adverse selection—the tendency for an individual who is aware of a pending loss to want insurance coverage, to a degree greater than one who is not aware of health problems or property conditions that have a chance of loss.

discrimination—the danger that refusing to grant policies in certain areas, or to people of certain economic or racial classes, is discriminatory and against the law.

substandard conditions—conditions that would increase risks to the insurer, and thus should be insured only for a higher rate than the typical individual or business.

uninsurable risks—identification of conditions that the insurer will not cover, under any circumstances.

See also *adverse selection; insurable risk; standard risk; substandard risk; underwriting; uninsurable risk.*

rollover IRA   an Individual Retirement Account (IRA) established to receive lump sum distributions from another account. The purpose of establishing such an IRA is to continue tax deferral rights. The individual will be taxed on distributed proceeds if the rollover account is not established within the time limit specified by law. Example: An employee who is fully vested in an employer's retirement account terminates employment, and is paid the account's value in a lump sum. The individual establishes a rollover IRA and deposits the proceeds in the account. As long as this is done within the time limit, none of the proceeds will be taxed. See also *Individual Retirement Account (IRA); lump sum distribution; qualified plan; retirement plan.*

S

safety   (1) the degree of protection afforded to the life, health, property and other interests of insured individuals, groups and businesses. The need for safety exists for the insured or for a beneficiary, depending on the type of loss being covered. (2) relative standard for selecting investments. Safety may be made a criteria in terms of the need for diversification or liquidity, protection of capital, or exposure to tax and inflation risk. See also *catastrophic loss; exposure to loss; investment income; risk.*

Savings Bank Life Insurance (SBLI)   a form of low-cost life insurance sold to customers in banks, avaiiable only in New York, Connecticut, and Massachusetts. See also *life insurance.*

savings element   the cash value that has built up in a whole life insurance policy, or the accumulated value of dividends in a participating life policy. As the duration of a policy's life increases, the savings element grows as well. For example, a whole life policy eventually consists entirely of the savings element, with the insurance portion reduced to zero. See also *cash value; dividend accumulation; life insurance; participating policy; whole life insurance.*

---

savings element

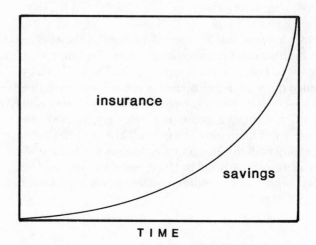

insurance

savings

T I M E

---

schedule rating   a technique used in setting rates for classes of coverage in some property and casualty insurance policies. Rates charged in subsequent policy years are modified based on actual loss experience, making a particular form of risk lower to the company. See also *experience rate; premium discount; property and casualty insurance; rate; retrospective rating.*

scheduled policy   a convenient form of property and casualty insurance, allowing the insured to select covered risks that would usually not be included. For example, a homeowner owns several pieces of rare art, furs and jewelry, or a stamp or coin collection. Any or all of these can be included in a scheduled policy for an additional annual premium. See also *exclusion; property and casualty insurance.* See illustration, page 189.

scheduled policy

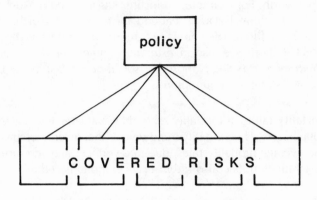

Section 401(k)   a section of the Internal Revenue Code defining the terms and conditions for an employer-sponsored retirement plan. A 401(k) plan allows employees to defer a limited amount of contributed annual income. See also *qualified plan; retirement plan; tax deferral.*

Section 403(b)   a section of the Internal Revenue Code defining provisions under which educational and qualified tax-exempt organizations may establish retirement plans for its employees. Contributions are applied toward the purchase of annuities for each qualified employee, subject to annual limitations. See also *annuity; qualified plan; retirement plan.*

Securities Investor Protection Corporation (SIPC)   an organization created by Congress in 1970 to provide insurance to investors. Accounts with securities broker-dealer members are insured against losses from failure of a brokerage firm or misuse of funds. However, insurance against investment losses is not provided. See also *investment income.*

securities valuation reserve   see   *Mandatory Securities Valuation Reserve (MSVR).*

security valuation methods   the rules applied in the valuation of securities held by insurance companies, based on guidelines established by the National Association of Insurance Commissioners (NAIC). The rules are conservative, for the purpose of stating an insurer's net worth at a reasonable level. Stocks are valued at market value as of the date of the financial statement.

Bond values depend on their rating, and are adjusted for purchase premium or discount. The valuation adjustment can make a significant difference in reported net worth. For example, an insurer has invested in stocks, with a cost basis of $13 million. But as of year-end, the market value of that portfolio has fallen to $10 million. The company is required to adjust its reported net worth by $3 million. See also *investment income; Mandatory Securities Valuation Reserve (MSVR); National Association of Insurance Commissioners (NAIC); statutory requirements.*

select mortality table   a mortality table that evaluates lives of recent insurance purchasers. The mortality trend reveals that recent purchasers have lower than average mortality rates, due to a younger age and more recent medical examination. See also *life insurance; mortality table.*

self-insurance   a form of allowing for risks by establishing reserves for future losses, as opposed to purchasing insurance protection. A group of companies may pool together to share risks, notably for low-severity losses. However, the same group may purchase outside insurance for high-severity losses. For example, a group of participating employers decides to provide group health insurance on a pooled basis, for all employees of the companies. As losses are submitted, they are paid from the pool. The employers have determined that the cost of funding and administering the pool is lower than insurance premiums for the same level of protection. However, the companies also pay group premiums for major medical insurance protection. See also *probability; risk.* See illustration, page 191.

Self-Insured Retention (SIR)   a form of self-insurance for property and casualty risks. The term is applied to limited losses on which the individual or company elects not to buy insurance, or to the deductible and coinsurance portions of existing coverage. See also *coinsurance; deductible; property and casualty insurance; risk.*

self-selection   adverse selection; the tendency of an individual to seek insurance in full knowledge of an illness and unfavorable conditions. The underwriting process is designed to uncover self-selection. If, however, the company discovers false statements have been made on an application, it may cancel the policy without paying a claim. See also *adverse selection; cancellation provision; risk; underwriting.*

separate account   an account established for a special purpose, such as a retirement fund or for the management and transaction of investment assets. See also *investment income; retirement plan.*

self-insurance

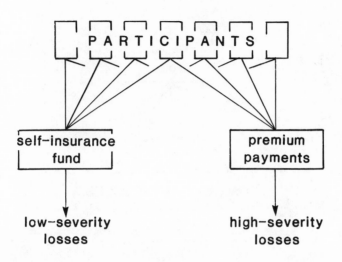

Servicemen's Group Life Insurance (SGLI)   a form of group term life insurance automatically provided to all members of the U.S. armed forces.
The policies are underwritten by commercial insurance companies on a
shared basis. Upon discharge from the armed forces, individuals have the
right to convert their SGLI policies to renewable term or permanent life insurance. See also *government life insurance; life insurance; term life*. See
illustration, page 192.

settlement   the payment or other application of benefit proceeds under a
contract of insurance. See also *benefit; claim; contract of insurance; optional settlement mode*.

settlement option   (1) the method of payment or application of the death
benefit under a life insurance contract. Proceeds may be paid in cash or used
in one of five optional modes:
   — left with the company, with interest to be paid to the beneficiary
periodically.
   — fixed amount payments, made on the basis of an agreed-upon rate
of interest, and lasting as long as proceeds are not depleted.
   — fixed period payments, the amount of each payment to be determined based on an agreed-upon rate of interest and the amount of proceeds.

Servicemen's Group Life Insurance (SGLI)

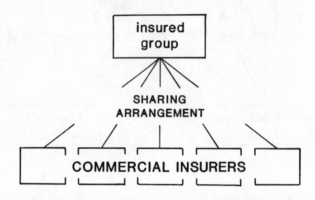

—life income, the creation of an annuity in which the death proceeds become a single premium.

(2) the method of application of policy dividends in a participating life policy. There are five possible modes of settlement:

—cash payment to the policyowner.

—reduction of premiums on the existing policy.

—purchase of paid-up additional life insurance.

—left with the company to accumulate at interest.

—applied toward the purchase of extended term insurance for a period of one year.

(3) the options available to the insurance company in the event of a casualty loss. The company may elect to:

—pay cash to reimburse the insured.

—take possession of the damaged property and replace it with other property.

—repair damaged property to serviceable condition.

See also *death benefit; dividend options; life insurance; optional settlement mode; participating policy; property and casualty insurance.* See illustrations, pages 193 and 194.

settlor   the individual who creates a trust. See also *trust.*

severity rate   the loss trend for a class of risks, based on the size of losses in a defined period of time. The trend is used as the basis for adjusting rates

settlement option (life)

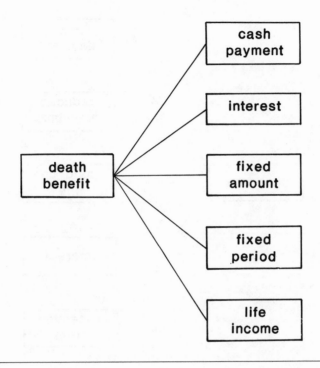

on similar policies to be written in the future. See also *loss trend; rate making.*

short-term disability   a disability, as defined in the insurance policy, that does not exceed a specified period, usually two years. See also *disability benefit; long-term disability.*

short-term insurance   insurance protection that remains in force for one year or less, such as extended term purchased as a settlement option. See also *extended term.*

Simplified Employee Pension plan (SEP)   a variation of the Individual Retirement Account (IRA) in which the employer makes contributions in behalf of each employee. The employee controls the investment directly, and all contributions are vested immediately. This plan can be used as an

settlement option (dividend)

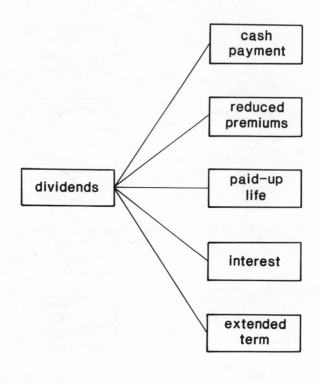

settlement option (casualty loss)

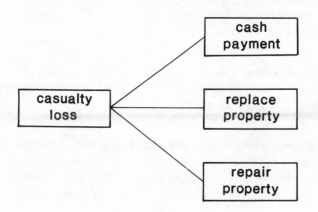

alternative to a 401(k) plan, or by a self-employed individual in place of a Keogh plan. See also *allocated benefits; immediate vesting; Individual Retirement Account (IRA); Keogh plan; qualified plan; retirement plan.*

single life annuity   an annuity in which benefits will be paid as long as the annuitant continues to live. In comparison, a joint life and survivors annuity calls for benefits to continue as long as either spouse is alive. See also *annuity; joint life and survivors annuity.*

---

single life annuity

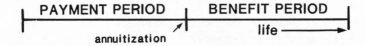

---

single premium deferred annuity   an annuity in which a one-time payment is made at the start of the contract term. After a deferral period, benefit payments begin and continue for life. See also *annuity; deferred annuity.*

---

single premium deferred annuity

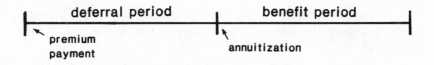

---

single premium life   life insurance in which a single premium is made at the time the contract is entered. The coverage period begins immediately and continues for the insured's life, without additional premiums paid. See also *life insurance; limited payment life; paid-up insurance; premium.* See illustration, page 196.

single premium life

sinking fund   a fund established to accumulate value over a period of time, to make payments in the future. Such a fund may be established for any purpose, such as payment of losses in a self-insured plan; savings for lump-sum payments of future premiums; or to protect against future temporary cash flow problems. See also *compound interest; present value; self-insurance.*

sliding scale commission   (1) payments to an agent that are based on the amount of insurance sold. For example, commissions on group insurance often are structured on the sliding scale basis. The percentage of commission is reduced with the volume sold to a group.

(2) a method of paying commissions paid by a reinsurer to the insurance company. The rate is reduced as an inversion of the ratio of losses paid. See also *commission; first year commission; group contract; reinsurance.*

Social Security Act of 1935   legislation that created the Social Security Administration and a range of public insurance and retirement benefits. In addition to Old Age, Survivors, Disability, and Health Insurance (OASDHI), the program has been supplemented with Medicare, payments of part of the health costs of retired Americans. Other major provisions of Social Security include:

—retirement benefits: paid to retired workers aged 65 and above (an optional, reduced benefit is available if the individual elects to begin receiving payments at age 62).

—survivorship benefit: paid to surviving spouses of workers, the monthly benefit dependent upon the number of dependent children in the household.

—disability benefit: payments to workers who are disabled and unable to work.

—health insurance: payments of health costs for those who cannot otherwise afford hospitalization and physician care, also called Medicaid; and Medicare, for part payment of costs for retired workers.

See also *disability income; health insurance; Medicaid; Medicare; Old*

Age, Survivors, Disability, and Health Insurance (OASDHI); retirement plan; survivorship benefit.

Social Security offset   a method for calculating retirement benefits, used in some plans. The total benefit, as calculated by formula, is reduced by the amount the individual is eligible to receive under the Social Security retirement program. See also *offset approach; retirement plan.*

Society of Actuaries (SA)   an organization whose members are actuaries in the insurance industry. The SA awards the designation Fellow, Society of Actuaries (FSA) upon successful completion of a series of examinations. See also *actuary; Fellow, Society of Actuaries (FSA).*

Society of Chartered Property and Casualty Underwriters (SCPCU)   an organization for underwriters in the property and casualty insurance industry. Individuals qualify for membership upon completion of a series of examinations administered by the American Institute for Property and Casualty Underwriters (AIPLU), and are awarded the CPCU designation. See also *American Institute for Property and Liability Underwriters (AIPLU); Chartered Property and Casualty Underwriter (CPCU); property and casualty insurance; underwriting.*

soliciting agent   the individual who identifies and contacts prospective purchasers of insurance policies. See also *agent; General Agent (GA); licensed agent.*

special agent   an agent authorized by the insurance company to sell policies in a territory, on an exclusive basis. See also *agent; exclusive agent.*

special mortality table   a mortality table used to compute rates on annuity contracts. The table is different from one used for life insurance, because the insurance company is underwriting a different risk. With life insurance, the risk is that the insured will die; with an annuity, the risk is that the insured will live (in which case, payments will continue for a longer than expected period of time). It is also assumed that annuitants generally will live longer than life insurance policyholders, and will tend to be in better health. See also *annuitant; mortality table.*

Special Multiperil Insurance (SMI)   business liability and casualty insurance offered through a single policy rather than a number of specialized ones, including several coverages:

     Property—Protection against losses to buildings and their contents, usually offered on an all risks basis.

Liability—Insurance for losses arising at business sites or for acts occurring while employees are away from the site on company business.

Crime—Protection against losses from employee theft, embezzlement, forgery and other, specified losses.

Machinery—Reimbursement for losses from explosion, accidents and other losses related to equipment and machinery.

See also *all risks; business liability; casualty insurance; liability insurance; property and casualty insurance.*

special risk (1) descriptive of an individual who, in the opinion of an underwriter, does not qualify for standard rates of insurance. This decision is based on a health condition, age, occupation, pre-existing conditions, hobbies, and other circumstances. A policy may be denied, offered at higher than the usual rate, or offered with specific risks excluded.

(2) a classification of risk that does not fit into a well understood pool of risks. For example, the risk of loss to a structure due to fire is one to which every property owner is exposed. But other forms of risk do not fit such categories, including coverages granted to entertainers, artists and athletes. See also *rated policy; risk; standard risk; underwriting.*

split dollar life an agreement for the purchase of whole life insurance, in which two people share the premium payments, most often an employer and employee. In the endorsement form of split dollar life, the employer owns the policy, and the employee has the right to select a beneficiary. In the collateral form, the employee is the owner, and premium payments made by the employer are to be treated as loans, and paid back in the future.

The employer's portion of payments is equal to the annual increase in cash value, and the balance of premiums is paid by the employee. Upon termination of employment, the employer has the option of selling the policy to the employee for the current cash value, or terminating the policy. In the event of the employee's death, the employer will be reimbursed for the amount of cash value, which increases during the term of insurance. The net proceeds will be paid to the beneficiary. See also *beneficiary; cash value; death benefit; life insurance; whole life insurance.*

split life a policy that includes elements of life insurance and an annuity. The premium paid for the annuity determines the amount of one-year renewable term insurance, which may be purchased by the annuitant. See also *annuity; life insurance.*

split limits limits placed on losses in property and casualty insurance policies. The limits are specified in terms of single events, a series of events, per person, and in dollar amounts. For example, an automobile policy includes the limits $100,000/300,000/50,000. The split limits are $100,000 maximum bodily injury per person; $300,000 total bodily injury per accident; and $50,000 total property damages per accident. See also *liability limits; property and casualty insurance.*

sprinkling trust   a trust allowing the trustee discretion to distribute assets to beneficiaries on the basis of need, or under guidelines established as part of the trust. See also *trust.*

standard form   an insurance policy containing provisions common to all similar policies. For example, the fire insurance policy contains clauses, limitations and exclusions that are similar or the same from one state to another. In addition, rates are set by each state on a uniform basis. See also *form; policy; rate.*

standard nonforfeiture   a clause providing that, upon termination of a life insurance policy, the minimum cash value must be paid. See also *cash value; life insurance; nonforfeiture provision.*

standard risk   an individual considered by the underwriter of an insurance company to be insurable at the usual rate. If the individual does not qualify, a policy may be offered at substandard rates; or the policy application may be denied. See also *risk; special risk; substandard risk; underwriting.*

standard valuation   the method, specified uniformly by the states, for calculating statutory reserves. See also *reserve value; statutory reserves; valuation reserve.*

state tax   any form of tax collected by the state. Insurance companies are not assessed an income or corporate tax, but pay a percentage of premiums. See also *premium tax.*

statutory accounting   the method for reporting assets, liabilities, equity, and operations in accordance with state law. Statutory accounting requires the establishment of reserves on a specific method of calculation; and the exclusion of certain assets as non-admitted. See also *annual statement; Commissioner of Insurance; convention blank; Generally Accepted Accounting Principles (GAAP).*

statutory earnings   earnings reported by insurance companies to the states, on a conservative basis. Reserves must be calculated at higher rates than would be dictated under Generally Accepted Accounting Principles

(GAAP), so that earnings are actually understated. See also *Generally Accepted Accounting Principles (GAAP); reserve value.*

statutory requirements the accounting rules applied by the National Association of Insurance Commissioners (NAIC) for uniform annual reporting by insurance companies. The cost of acquiring new business must be written off during the year acquired (under GAAP rules, commissions and other costs are amortized over the expected policy life). And statutory reserves are higher than GAAP reserves, resulting in lower reported profits. See also *Generally Accepted Accounting Principles (GAAP); National Association of Insurance Commissioners (NAIC); reserve value.*

statutory reserves conservatively established reserves, required of insurance companies for the purpose of establishing net worth and reporting annual or quarterly results. The purpose of conservative reserve valuation is to ensure that the company remains financially able to pay all future claims. See also *Loss Frequency Method (LFM); reserve.*

stepped-up basis a calculation of property value as of the time of death. The purpose is to establish value for the purpose of estate taxes. In addition, the stepped-up basis serves as the original basis for individuals inheriting that property. For example, an individual purchased real estate many years ago, paying $15,000. As of the time of death, the property is appraised for $210,000. That will represent the stepped-up basis. The profit, $195,000, is subject to estate taxes. The heir receives the property with the $195,000 stepped-up basis, and later sells it. The heir's capital gain is the difference between the sale price and the stepped-up basis. See also *estate tax.*

stock company an insurance company that has issued stock, and is owned collectively by stockholders. In comparison, a mutual company is owned by policyholders in proportion to the size of their policies. See also *mutual company.*

stop loss reinsurance a form of agreement between an insurance company and a reinsurer, limiting the aggregate amount of losses that must be shared during a specified period of time. While the reinsurance company accepts individual risks, it will not be required to pay claims above the aggregate limit. For example, a company cedes insurance above its retention limit, and also provides a stop loss limitation. If actual losses reach that level, the reinsurer will not be required to pay any further claim. See also *excess of loss plan; quota share reinsurance; percentage participating deductible; reinsurance; retention.*

straight deductible   a deductible computed on an unchanging basis; either a fixed dollar deductible or a percentage of all losses. While the latter is more accurately called coinsurance, it is sometimes referred to as a percentage deductible. For example, one policy has a $100 deductible. All claims will be reduced by that amount, and the balance paid. Another policy has a percentage deductible of 10%. All claims will be 90% paid, and the policyholder will be responsible for the 10% balance. See also *deductible; disappearing deductible.*

straight life annuity   see   *life annuity certain.*

straight life insurance   see   *ordinary life.*

straight term life   see   *term life.*

subrogation   the right of an insurer to seek reimbursement of paid losses, when a third party is responsible. For example, a company pays a covered loss to an insured, which was caused by another property owner. Under the subrogation clause, the company may seek reimbursement of its payment from that person. See also *contract of insurance; policy; property and casualty insurance.*

subscriber   an individual who belongs to a group hospitalization plan. See also *group health; health insurance.*

substandard life   a health or life insurance policy issued at higher than standard rates, because the insured was considered a greater than average risk. See also *health insurance; life insurance; risk.*

substandard risk   an individual who does not meet the qualifications for standard policy rates. The company will either offer a policy at higher premium rates, or will decline to provide coverage. See also *impaired risk; risk; standard risk.*

substantial owner limitation   a ceiling placed on the total amount of benefits that can be accrued by and paid to principals in a business, under the terms of a qualified retirement plan. A substantial owner may be someone who owns 5% or more of the stock, is paid $75,000 or more per year, or is paid $50,000 or more when that is in the top 20% of salaries paid. See also *qualified plan; retirement plan.*

suicide clause   a clause in all life insurance policies specifying that no death benefit will be paid if the insured commits suicide within the first two years of the policy term. This is aimed at eliminating the purchase of insurance in contemplation of suicide. In the event of suicide, the company will cancel the policy and return all premiums paid to date, to the beneficiary. See also *adverse selection; cancellation provision; life insurance.*

supplemental disability a disability defined by the Social Security administration, for the purpose of computing benefits. This applies when other benefits are already being paid. For example, a retired worker is receiving old age benefits, and his spouse is disabled. The amount of benefit to be paid will be based on the retired worker's qualification level. See also *disability income; Social Security Act of 1935.*

supplementary contract insurance created by the application of death proceeds or dividend accumulations. Rather than taking payments in cash, the policyowner elects to apply dividends (or, the beneficiary elects to apply all or part of the death proceeds) to premium payments on new insurance. See also *death benefit; dividend; life insurance; optional settlement mode; settlement option.*

Surety Association of America (SAA) an association for companies and employees of companies that market surety bonds. See also *bond.*

surety bond a guarantee made by one person or company. In the event of a failure to perform, the guarantor agrees to make payment. See also *bond.*

surplus line a form of insurance that is not offered by a company admitted to conduct business in the applicant's state. Under that condition, the agent may apply for coverage from a non-admitted company. See also *admitted company; non-admitted company.*

surplus reinsurance an agreement creating a form of automatic reinsurance. The writing company agrees to cede risks above a predetermined retention limit, and the reinsurer agrees to accept those risks. For example, an insurer has a retention limit of $25,000, so that it will not assume risks above that level. An application for a $100,000 policy is approved. The company cedes the $75,000 above its retention limit, under a surplus reinsurance agreement. See also *life insurance; reinsurance; retention.*

surrender fee a fee charged to a policyholder of an individual or group life insurance policy, or an annuity, for surrendering within a specified time period. This is a form of back-end load. For example, cash value currently is $880, and a provision of the policy stipulates that 10% is to be paid as a surrender fee. The company deducts $88 and remits the balance to the policyholder. See also *annuity; back-end load; cash value; life insurance.*

surrender value   the current cash value of a whole life insurance policy or an annuity, to be paid to a policyholder in the event the policy is terminated. See also *annuity; cash value; life insurance; nonforfeiture provision; whole life insurance.*

survivorship annuity   **(1)** an annuity based on the lives of two spouses. Monthly benefits are to be paid for as long as either spouse is alive.

   (2) an annuity created at the point of the death of an insured, with all or part of the death benefit used to fund payments to a beneficiary. See also *annuity; joint life and survivors annuity; life insurance; reversionary interest.*

survivorship annuity (joint)

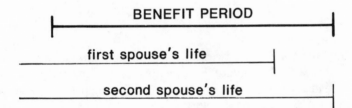

survivorship annuity (life)

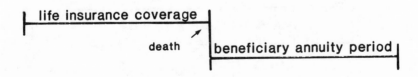

survivorship life   a type of life insurance policy based on the mortality of both spouses. A benefit is to be paid only upon the death of the last surviving spouse. This type of policy might be purchased to fund payments of estate taxes, or to eliminate debts at the point of death. See also *death benefit; estate planning; joint life and survivors insurance; life insurance.*

---

survivorship life

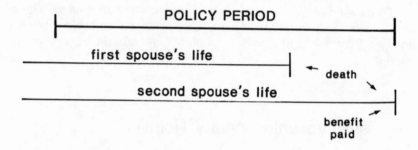

---

syndicate a pool formed by several participants, to share the risks or benefits of a particular venture. For example, several insurance companies participate in a pool to share the risks of policies written above the retention limits of each. See also *pool; reinsurance; risk; underwriting.*

---

syndicate

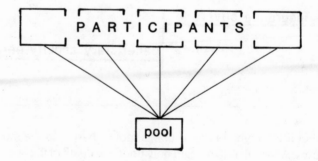

T

tabular interest rate   the rate used in calculation of a policy's reserve. The assumption regarding future earnings on investments will affect today's reserve, which represents the estimate of present value of future claims. See also *interest rate; present value; reserve.*

tabular mortality   in life insurance, the rate of deaths assumed to occur at a specified age, based on the mortality table in use. See also *life insurance; mortality.*

tail coverage   a special form of liability insurance that continues in force beyond the final date of another liability policy. Its purpose is to protect the insured against losses arising from events that occurred during the policy period. In claims occurrence insurance policies, no benefits will be paid after termination date. See also *claims occurrence insurance; long-tail liability; property and casualty insurance.*

tail coverage

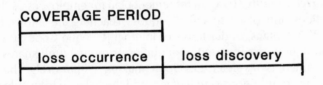

target benefit plan   a form of retirement plan in which a specific amount of benefit is determined in advance, and contributions for each employee are made in accordance with that calculation. It includes an assumption of interest, the amount of contribution, and the number of years until planned retirement date. See also *defined benefit plan; pension plan; retirement plan.*

tax deferral   the investing of money in such a way that income (or, in some instances, the invested funds) will not be taxed until a later date. One example is whole life insurance. Cash values accumulate over the policy period, and are not taxed as ordinary income in the year earned. The Individual Retirement Account (IRA) and Keogh plan are forms of tax deferral plans. Contributions are exempt from taxes during the year made. (Note: The Tax Reform Act of 1986 excluded IRA contributions from tax deferral if the individual earns income in excess of certain levels, or participates in another qualified plan.) A self-employed individual may save 20% of annual net profits (before computing the Keogh contribution) each year, exempting the entire contribution and all earnings from tax. See also *financial plan; Individual Retirement Account (IRA); Keogh plan; retirement plan.*

tax deferral

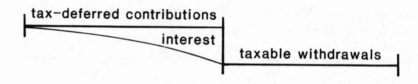

Tax-Deferred Annuity (TDA)   a retirement plan for employees of charitable organizations and other specified groups. Teachers are allowed to participate in TDA plans, under terms of Internal Revenue Code 501(c)(3).

Contributions are invested in annuities or mutual fund shares, and all income earned is tax-deferred. Upon making withdrawals, the portion representing contributions is free of tax, and the balance is taxable. The exclusion ratio applied to each withdrawal is computed based on the individual's age, life expectancy, and the expected rate of return. See also *annuity; exclusion ratio; Section 403(b).* See illustration, page 207.

Tax Equity and Fiscal Responsibility Act of 1982 (TEFRA)   federal tax legislation that modified rules and qualifications for tax shelters; changed the computation of taxes on life insurance earnings; and limited tax-free withdrawals from annuity plans. See also *annuity; life insurance.*

tax-free rollover   the transfer of funds in a tax-deferred plan to a subsequent plan. When transferring vested payments from an employer's plan, for example, an employee must establish a rollover IRA and deposit the funds within 60 days from the date funds were paid out. The rollover should not

Tax-Deferred Annuity (TDA)'

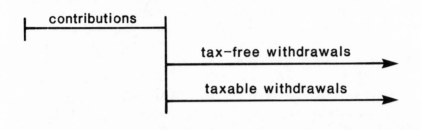

contributions

tax-free withdrawals

taxable withdrawals

---

be confused with the transfer, in which funds from one IRA are moved to another, or when two IRA plans are consolidated. See also *Individual Retirement Account (IRA); retirement plan; rollover IRA.*

tax multiplier   the rate that is paid in premium tax, as applied to the gross premium actually charged. In most states, the premium tax rate is 2%. Thus, a gross premium will be increased by the amount of the tax multiplier. To compute the amount of increase, the gross premium before premium taxes is divided by the inversion of the tax rate. The result is the amount of gross premium, and is subject to the percentage of tax. For example, a premium before computation of premium taxes is $407.90 per year. That amount, divided by .98, is $416.22. To prove this calculation, multiply by the rate, 2%. The result is the amount of premium tax liability, $8.32, and the remaining balance, $407.90, is the gross premium before taxes. See also *gross premium; premium tax.*

tax planning   the anticipation of tax liabilities, and timing of actions to reduce or eliminate the amount that must be paid. Examples include investing funds in tax-deferred accounts; timing business expenses; and selecting certain types of insurance products. See also *estate planning; financial plan.*

Tax Reform Act of 1984   federal tax legislation that limited the tax benefits of borrowing cash value, and increased taxes on insurance company profits. See also *cash value; life insurance.*

Tax Reform Act of 1986   federal tax legislation that eliminated the majority of tax shelter benefits in investments defined as passive. Tax rates were reduced and simplified, and a number of deductions previously allowed were eliminated or reduced. The exclusion from current tax of contributions to an Individual Retirement Account (IRA) was reduced when annual income for an individual exceeds $35,000 ($50,000 ceiling for a married couple), and completely eliminated for those participating in a separate qualified plan. This law also defined "highly compensated employee" for the purpose of identifying top-heavy plans. See also *Individual Retirement Account (IRA); qualified plan; top-heavy plan.*

Tax-Sheltered Annuity (TSA) a form of retirement plan especially for employees of certain institutions, such as public schools. The TSA is defined under Internal Revenue Code Section 501(c)(3). See also *Tax-Deferred Annuity (TDA).*

temporary license a license to sell insurance for a limited period of time, usually six months or less. It is issued in many states, pending successful completion of a state-administered examination for a permanent salesperson's license. See also *agent; licensed agent.*

temporary life annuity any form of annuity in which benefit payments will continue until the annuitant dies, but for no longer than a specified period of time. For example, a contract promises to continue payments for life or 10 years, whichever occurs first. In one plan, the annuitant dies after seven years, and benefits cease immediately. In another plan, the individual lives beyond the 10-year date. Benefits cease at the conclusion of the tenth year. See also *annuity.*

---

temporary life annuity

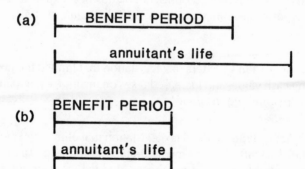

tenancy by the entirety a form of ownership in which a married couple own property jointly. In the event of death, the ownership automatically passes over to the surviving spouse. This form of ownership may be in effect for individuals other than married couples, too. For example, a partnership with three owners is registered as a tenancy by the entirety. If one partner dies, that portion of total equity will be split between the surviving partners. See also *Joint Tenancy With Rights of Survivorship (JTWROS)*.

---

tenancy by
the entirety

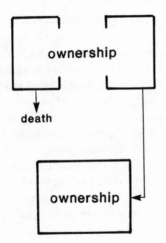

ownership

death

ownership

---

tenants in common a form of ownership in which a married couple owns property jointly. However, in the event of the death of one spouse, that portion of ownership passes to the individual's heirs, and not to the surviving spouse. This form of ownership may be used in jointly owned properties by individuals other than married couples. For example, three partners each own one-third of the business. If registered as a tenancy in common, the one-third ownership of a deceased partner passes to that partner's heirs, and not the surviving owners. See also *ownership rights*. See illustration, page 210.

tenants in common

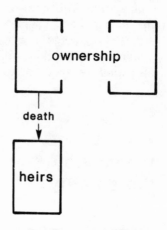

ownership

death

heirs

---

term life   a form of life insurance that provides protection only, with no accruing cash values, policy dividends, or other savings elements. There are two broad forms of term coverage. First is level term, in which the amount of insurance does not change. At the end of a specified term of years, the policy may be renewed; however, premiums will be increased based on the insured person's attained age. Second is decreasing term life, in which the amount of insurance in force declines over the term. However, the amount of premium payments remains unchanged. Certain decreasing term policies allow the insured to convert a policy to another type of insurance, at which time premiums will be adjusted. See also *attained age; decreasing term life; in force; level term; life insurance.* See illustration, page 211.

terminal dividend   the final dividend due and payable under the terms of a participating life policy, either upon termination or maturity. A terminal dividend may also be declared by the company, to be paid after termination of a number of years, and representing a share of profits above the company's expectations. See also *dividend; life insurance; participating policy.*

terminal reserve   the life insurance reserve as of the end of the policy year. It is calculated based on actuarial assumptions, premium payments, and the age of the insured. The terminal reserve is used in calculation of the mean reserve (initial plus terminal reserve, divided by two). See also *initial reserve; life insurance; mean reserve; reserve.*

term life

LEVEL TERM

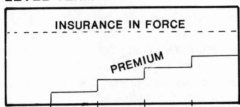

DECREASING TERM

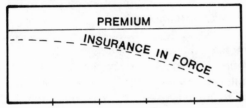

---

termination the end of a contract of insurance, resulting from one of seven events:

— cancellation by the insurance company, due to discovered misrepresentations or fraud, or by exercising a policy provision allowing termination due to other circumstances.

— non-payment of premiums by the insured.

— maturity of the policy.

— death of the insured, if a life insurance policy, after which a death benefit is paid.

— surrender of the policy for cash value.

— expiration of a term, applicable in term life insurance, annuities, and other forms of coverage with defined terms of years.

— conversion from one policy to another.

See also *cancellation provision; lapse.*

termination rate a trend in lapses of policies in force, also called the Lapse Ratio (LR). The level and volume of terminations are one factor used in establishing reserve and premium levels. See also *Lapse Ratio (LR; premium; reserve.*

testamentary trust   a trust established as part of a deceased person's will. Upon death, property is transferred to the trustee's control. Terms of the will dictate how and when property is to be distributed to heirs. See also *trust; will.*

testator   the individual who draws a will. See also *estate planning; will.*

Three Factor Contribution Method (TFCM)   a method used in the calculation of dividends in participating policies. The factors are mortality, expenses and the assumed rate of interest. See also *dividend; expense load; interest rate; mortality; participating policy.*

threshold level   the minimum level of loss or injury at which a damaged person may sue. The threshold is defined in terms of dollar amount of the loss, the period of disability, or type of injury suffered. See also *liability; property and casualty insurance.*

time value of money   the relative value when the factor of time is added to rate and amount. For example, a six percent return for one compound period yields only six percent. When interest is compounded over many periods, the total return increases each year. This is due to the effect of paying or receiving interest on interest. For example, an individual deposits $100 in an account, with compounding to be calculated on a quarterly basis at 6%. At the end of the first year, the account's value has risen to $106.14. However, after 10 years, the account's value will have risen to $181.40. Time value of money calculations occurs in a number of ways, including the present and accumulated value of a sum.

The example above is of the "accumulated value of 1," meaning the amount to which a single sum of money will grow over time, assuming a rate, compound method, and number of periods. A series of deposits will accumulate to a different amount, and are called the "accumulated value of 1 per period." The reverse calculation is present value. To determine the amount required to build to a predetermined amount in the future, it is necessary to calculate the "present value of 1," with assumptions about the rate of interest, compound method, and number of periods. If a series of deposits are made, the calculation is called the "present value of 1 per period." See also *accumulated value; compound interest; interest; present value.* See illustration, page 213.

title insurance   a form of insurance for property buyers, against the contingency that an outstanding lien or other encumbrance has been placed on the property. Encumbrances are secured by title to property, regardless of the current owner. For example, an individual purchases a house, not

time value of money

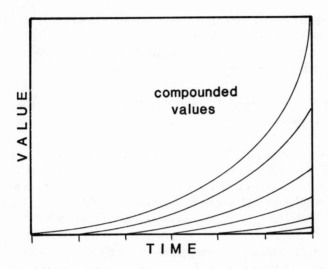

knowing that the previous owner borrowed $50,000 and pledged that property as security. Upon issuing a title insurance policy, the company investigates the chain of title, and attempts to discover all existing and unpaid liens. If, however, the company fails to discover the outstanding lien, the homeowner will be protected and will not be required to satisfy the debt. A title insurance policy requires a single payment at the time the coverage is bought, and it remains in effect for as long as the individual owns the property. See also *real property.*

top-heavy plan any qualified profit-sharing or pension plan that favors highly-compensated employees or controlling officers. Under provisions of the Tax Reform Act of 1986, a highly compensated employee is defined as anyone who (a) owns or controls 5% or more of the company's stock or equity; (b) receives $75,000 or more in annual compensation; (c) receives $50,000 or more in annual compensation and is among the 20% highest paid employees; or (d) is an officer whose total compensation exceeds defined contribution limits by 150% or more. See also *qualified plan; retirement plan; Tax Reform Act of 1986.*

tort law a classification of law defining civil wrongful acts, apart from criminal acts. A tort may involve negligence, intentional interference, absolute liability, or strict liability. See also *absolute liability; liability; negligence.*

total disability any condition that prevents an insured individual from performing the normal duties and acts required in his or her job, or in a job for which that person is reasonably qualified. See also *disability; health insurance; partial disability.*

total loss a loss in which property cannot be repaired or partially saved. See also *catastrophic loss; loss.*

total needs a marketing technique used to sell life and disability insurance. The family's total needs are estimated, allowing for a spouse's ability to earn a living; Social Security benefits; and other assets and sources of income. In a complete total needs analysis, both life and disability risks are considered. See also *disability income; life insurance; needs approach.*

treasury stock stock that a corporation buys back, and then classifies as authorized but unissued stock. The stock may be reissued at a later date, or retired. See also *equity; net worth; stock company.*

treaty a reinsurance agreement between two or more companies. One company, the ceding insurer, will grant a reinsurer a portion of all premiums it receives for those portions of policies that are ceded. In return, the reinsurer agrees to pay for its share of claims on the same risks. See also *reinsurance treaty; retention.*

---

treaty

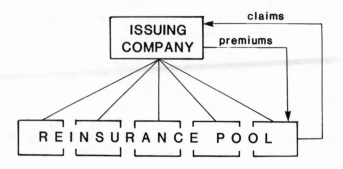

true group plan   a group insurance plan in which one master policy is sold, and certificates of insurance are given to each covered individual. In comparison, "groups" may be granted similar coverages under a wholesale plan, and each receives a separate policy. Although this is a group, it is not a group in the true sense, because different contracts are drawn for each covered person. See also *certificate of insurance; group contract; master policy; wholesale life.*

---

true group plan

---

trust   a vehicle for the temporary transfer of ownership in property, from the settlor (creator of the trust) to the trustee. The trustee managed property in behalf of the beneficiary, performing as fiduciary, and will eventually transfer title to beneficiaries in accordance with the terms of the trust. See also *beneficiary; estate planning; fiduciary; settlor.*

trust indenture   the trust contract, or document specifying the terms of a trust. It specifies the duties and restrictions of the trustee, the rights of beneficiaries, and method and timing of distributions. See also *contract; fiducicary; settlor.*

Trust Indenture Act of 1939   legislation that spells out the method by which corporate bonds and other securities may be issued. This law specifies the fiduciary responsibilities of the individual who manages the issue and makes distributions. See also *fiduciary; investment income.*

turnover rate   the rate of employee terminations, calculated for the purpose of calculating and adjusting retirement plan values and payments. For example, a plan is initiated with the idea that upon reaching age 65, employees will begin receiving benefits. However, some employees must be expected to leave employment before that date. All vested portions of contributions made until the time of termination must be paid out to those employees. There are two considerations in the adjustment: First is allowing for payments of vested portions; second is a calculation of the unvested values, which accrue to the benefit of remaining employees. See also *actuarial adjustments; retirement plan; vesting.*

twisting   the unethical practice among agents of replacing one insurance policy for another. The purpose is to produce a new first year commission, when the commission rate is substantially higher than renewal rates. Twisting occurs in one of two ways. The agent either induces individuals to replace an existing policy, written with another company, with a new policy; or, the agent argues for replacement of a policy that he or she sold to the policyholder in the past. See also *commission; first year commission; life insurance; replacement.*

U

ultimate mortality table   a mortality table that includes probability factors on the lives of insured individuals beyond the first five to ten years a policy is in force. The purpose is to allow for the overall lower mortality rates among those who recently purchased life insurance. See also *life insurance; mortality table; select mortality table.*

umbrella policy   a business liability policy that offers protection above the policy limits of other, existing policies. The purpose is to protect against losses that are uncovered in standard contracts. See also *blanket contract; Business Owner's Policy (BOP); liability insurance.* See illustration, page 217.

umbrella reinsurance   forms of property and casualty insurance that combine coverages for a range of risks. This arrangement allows the writing company to spread its risks efficiently. For example, an insurer is exposed to a number of risks above retention limits. Under the terms of an umbrella

umbrella policy

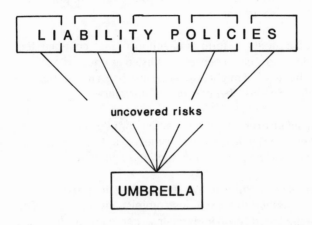

---

reinsurance treaty, other insurers agree to accept a fixed percentage of all risks in a defined range. Thus, reinsurers may not select the least severe forms of risk, and exclude other forms. See also *property and casualty insurance; reinsurance; retention.*

---

umbrella reinsurance

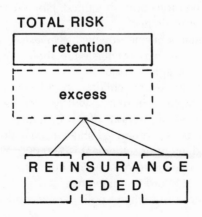

umpire clause   a contractual statement in which both sides agree to settle disputes through arbitration. Rather than resorting to litigation, the parties to the contract will abide by the final decision of appointed arbitrators or umpires. See also *arbitration.*

unallocated benefits   a form of health insurance coverage for various and miscellaneous hospital expenses. Not listed as covered nor as excluded services, the charges that might arise are paid up to a maximum under the terms of the policy. See also *benefit; health insurance.*

unauthorized insurer   also called a non-admitted company, an insurer that has not been licensed to conduct business in a state. See also *admitted company; authorized company; non-admitted company.*

unbundled plan   administrative services that are provided to a self-insured group, or insurance that excludes administrative services. For example, a group of self-insured companies retains a company to administer claims. See also *Administrative Services Only (ASO); risk management; self-insurance.*

under-insurance   **(1)** status of a company, individual or property that is inadequately protected. Whenever a loss would create economic consequences that could not be borne, or that would create a significant hardship, the need for insurance is apparent. Examples:
  —an individual is the sole supporter of a spouse and several children. In the event of death, the family would not be able to continue mortgage payments on the home, nor to meet its monthly expenses. Without life insurance, this individual is under-insured.
  —a married couple is purchasing a home, and both work. Two incomes are required in order to meet monthly expenses. In the event of disability of either individual, the family budget could not be met. In this situation, disability income protection is required. Not to carry such policies is another case of under-insurance.
  —an individual or business owner has invested thousands of dollars in property. If that property was lost due to fire, theft, or other casualties, the owner could not afford replacement.
  —a family with several children could not afford an extended hospital visit. Major medical insurance will protect the family against the economic consequences of a serious illness or injury.
  —a professional is exposed to liability from malpractice suits. In his state, the average judgment or settlement is $50,000. Yet, his malpractice coverage provides a maximum of only $10,000. The individual is under-insured if he could not afford the difference.
  (2) a condition that arises when a policy covers only a portion of losses,

requiring the insured individual or business to provide coinsurance. If that individual could not afford the loss, the coinsurance requirement has not been met.

See also *coinsurance; over-insurance.*

underwriting **(1)** risk selection; the process of evaluating applications for insurance, and determining the degree of risk to which the company is exposed. The underwriter must be able to discover conditions revealed in the application, the medical exam (in cases of life and health underwriting), and the conditions adding to risk. In property insurance, the underwriting process must evaluate risks based on area, special circumstances, and liability limits.

(2) name often used to describe the process of selling insurance, preferred by some to the title of salesperson. Use of the name underwriter implies a higher level of sophistication. However, this usage is misleading and confusing.

See also *adverse selection; agency; risk selection.*

underwriting cycle the tendency of premium levels to rise and fall in a predictable pattern over time. As underwriting standards are tightened (in response to higher than expected losses), premium rates rise. This creates greater income and a corresponding drop in losses. At this point, underwriting standards are loosened, and losses then rise to complete the cycle. The cycle is more descriptive in terms of premiums for property and casualty insurance than for other forms of insurance. See also *losses incurred; property and casualty insurance; premium.*

underwriting gain/loss the profit or loss that results from the writing of insurance policies. Companies have two sources of income: from underwriting and from investments. The gain is the amount of premiums earned, minus all claims, commissions, and other costs paid. A loss occurs when expenses and claims exceed premium earnings. Example: One company reports a loss in underwriting activity for the year. However, investment net income is greater than the underwriting loss, so that the company reports an overall net profit. See also *investment net income; loss.*

unearned premium the portion of premiums received that apply to later periods. The company does not recognize these payments as "earned" until the applicable period of coverage. For example, the insured pays an annual premium of $1,200 at the beginning of the policy year. One-twelfth, or $100, will become earned each month. Thus, in the first month, the company records the receipt as $100 of earned and $1,100 of unearned premium. See also *earned premium; modal premium; premium; written premium.*

underwriting cycle

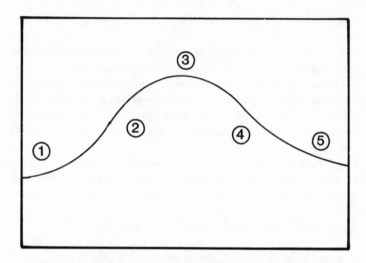

1 underwriting standards are tightened
2 premium rates increase
3 profits rise as losses decline
4 underwriting standards are loosened
5 profits fall as losses increase

unearned premium

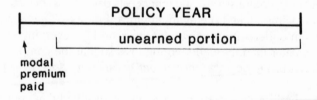

unearned premium reserve a reserve for the unearned portion of premiums that have been received prior to the period in which risks exist. In the event of cancellation of a policy, the unearned portion of premiums is returned to the policyholder. The reserve is established to create a liability for this, and is based on estimates developed from historical cancellations and terminations. For example, a company has experienced a 12 termination rate during the first year a new policy is written. It establishes an unearned premium reserve equal to 12% of all first-year premiums paid. Additional reserve calculations are made for subsequent policy year payments of modal premium. See also *earned premium; premium; reserve.*

unemployment compensation insurance provided by a payroll tax assessed against employers, and based on the level of compensation to employees. In cases of involuntary termination, the insurance provides for monthly unemployment payments. The tax is collected on the state and federal levels, and was originally created as part of the Social Security system. See also *employee; Social Security Act of 1935.*

uniform forms standard forms, the collective terms and conditions of insurance policies that are used widely. See also *form; standard form.*

Uniform Gift to Minors Act (UGMA) a section of the Internal Revenue Code specifying conditions under which gifts to children will not be subject to gift taxes. See also *financial plan; tax planning.*

Uniform Individual Accident and Sickness Policy Provisions Act (UIASPPA) a regulation published by the National Association of Insurance Commissioners (NAIC) setting down minimum provisions that must be included in all individual health insurance policies. See also *health insurance; National Association of Insurance Commissioners (NAIC).*

Uniform Reciprocal Licensing Act (URLA) a law at the state level that regulates the activities of non-admitted companies. Among other provisions, it provides for revocation of a home-state license when a non-admitted company conducts business in a state where it is not licensed. See also *foreign company; non-admitted company.*

Uniform Simultaneous Death Act (USDA) a law at the state level defining procedures for payments of life insurance benefits in the event of a common disaster. For example, a husband carries a life insurance policy in which his wife is named as beneficiary, and the children as contingent beneficiaries. Both husband and wife die at the same time, in a common disaster. The law states that in this event, it will be presumed that the beneficiary died before the insured. Benefits will be paid to the contingent beneficiary. If none is named in the policy, benefits will go to the insured's estate. See also *beneficiary; common disaster clause; contingent beneficiary; insured.*

unilateral contract a contract in which only one side promises to perform. An insurance contract, in most instances, is unilateral. For example, the company agrees to pay benefits in cases of covered losses. The insured may keep the policy in force by making the required premium payments, but is not contractually obligated to keep the policy in force. The insurance contract becomes bilateral in cases where the insured is required to perform in some way. For example, a casualty insurance policy specifies that the insured is required to install and monitor safety procedures, as a condition for continued favorable rates. See also *bilateral contract; contract.*

uninsurable risk a risk that the insurance company determines is unacceptance, as defined by its underwriting standards.

Example: An individual applying for life insurance is an uninsurable risk if the medical examination reveals a terminal condition; if that individual has specific, chronic health conditions; or if he or she is in a particularly hazardous occupation.

Example: A health insurance company receives an application from an individual, and the application reveals a history of respiratory problems. The application may be denied, or the company will offer one that specifically names respiratory conditions as exclusions from coverage.

See also *insurable risk; risk; substandard risk.*

uninsured motorist coverage in a Personal Automobile Policy (PAP) providing for losses when another motorist does not carry liability insurance. See also *liability insurance; Personal Automobile Policy (PAP).*

unit annuity a form of annuity in which units are purchased each year. The amount is normally fixed, and the number of units purchased varies, based on variable costs and profits, the annuitant's age, and life expectancy. Unit annuities usually are used as part of a group annuity plan, as part of a retirement arrangement through an employer. See also *annuity; group annuity; variable dollar annuity.*

unit benefit plan a form of retirement plan in which the amount of annual retirement benefit is calculated by means of a formula. Involved are the years of service, an annual "unit" value, and average earnings during a defined period of time (the last year worked, or the average of the last several years). For example, one plan accumulates 1¼% for each year of service. During the final five years of employment, one individual earns average compensation of $80,000, and was employed for a total of 23 years. The annual benefit is $23,000:

years	×	units	×	earnings	=	benefit
23	×	1.25%	×	$80,000	=	$23,000

unit annuity

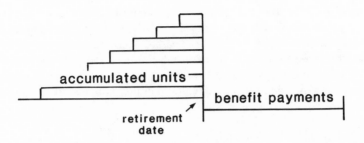

accumulated units

benefit payments

retirement
date

unit benefit plan

years of service	x	annual unit	x	average earnings

23 x 1.25% x $80,000 = $23,000

United States Government Life Insurance (USGLI)   a program established in 1919, that provided up to $10,000 in renewable term life insurance to members of the U.S. armed forces. This program was replaced in 1940 by the National Service Life Insurance (NSLI) program. See also *government life insurance; group life; life insurance; renewable term life.*

universal life   a form of life insurance that combines accumulating cash value with a varying rate of return. After the initial premium has been paid, the insured decides when to make a subsequent payment (subject to minimum requirements). Payments of premium increase cash value, and the insurer's pure cost of providing insurance is deducted.

The universal life plan provides flexible levels of coverage for flexible premium amounts. In the event the insured desires to increase the death benefit level, the company may require evidence of insurability. See also *adjustable life; cash value; evidence of insurability; flexible premium life; life insurance; variable life; whole life insurance.*

universal variable life   a form of universal life in which the amount added to cash value varies each year. The variation depends on the profits or losses from investments made through a separate account. Example: A contract allows the policyholder to choose from among a group of mutual funds. Cash payments are invested in those funds each year. If those funds report higher than expected profits, cash value will increase accordingly. See also *investment income; variable life.*

unreported claim   a claim that has occurred, but has not yet been reported to the insurer. At the end of each reporting period, the insurance company must estimate the level of claims, and establish a reserve to allow for those claims. See also *claim; Incurred But Not Reported (IBNR).*

unsolicited application   an application for insurance coverage that is received by the company not through an agent, but directly. In life and health insurance companies, the underwriter will examine the application more carefully than one solicited through an agent, on the presumption that the insured may desire insurance because he or she is aware of an unfavorable health condition. See also *adverse selection; application; risk selection; self-selection; underwriting.*

Usual, Customary and Reasonable (UCR)   a term in health insurance policies, stating that the company will reimburse covered expenses only to the extent that such charges do not exceed the going rates. See also *health insurance.*

V

valid contract   a contract that meets all of the requirements of law, and contains no unenforceable or illegal clauses; is entered into by individuals capable of making a contract; contains consideration; and results from a meeting of the minds of both parties. See also *contract; void contract.*

validation period   the period of time required for a life insurance company to amortize its cost of acquiring new business. This period may extend as long as 10 years from the date a policy is initiated. For example, one line of insurance includes a first-year commission rate of 240%. For every $100 collected, the agent is paid $240. In addition, the company must allow for its administrative costs.

On a statutory reporting basis, the company is required to absorb first-year expenses during the first year. When earnings are restarted on a (Generally Accepted Accounting Principles (GAAP) basis, first-year acquisition expenses are amortized over the validation period. See also *first year commission; GAAP requirements; life insurance; load; new business; statutory requirements.*

---

validation period

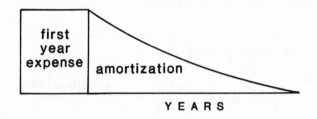

YEARS

---

valuation method   (1) the method employed to determine the amount of a covered loss, for the purposes of property and casualty insurance. Example: An individual files a claim with the insurance company. An adjuster evaluates the loss by visiting the site, and computes the value.

(2) In life insurance, the method used to calculate policy reserves.

(3) In settling an estate, the method used to place current market values on properties. This is for the purpose of calculating the stepped-up basis of appreciated property, and for calculating estate taxes.

See also *adjuster; estate tax; life insurance; loss; property and casualty insurance; reserve value; stepped-up basis.*

valuation premium   the method of determining premium, based on required reserve levels. States set reserve standards for policies, so that the indicated levels must be used in setting reasonable net premium rates. Because state standards are conservative, companies sometimes establish gross premium at levels below the required net premium reserve level; in this case, the difference must be offset in a deficiency reserve. See also *deficiency reserve; life insurance; premium; rate; reserve.*

valuation reserve (1) the reserve established on the basis of state standards, used to determine valuation premium.

(2) an amount set up as a liability to adjust for differences between book value and current market value of an asset. See also *reserve.*

variable dollar annuity an annuity contract in which annual units are purchased, often through a retirement plan account. The number of units varies with unit cost. At the time of annuitization, the accumulated unit value determines the level of periodic benefit payments that will be made. See also *annuity; retirement plan; unit annuity.*

variable dollar annuity

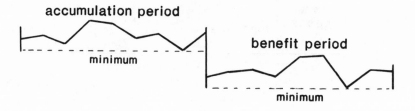

variable life a form of whole life insurance in which the cash value varies, depending on investment performance in a separate account. The company guarantees a minimum death benefit, and gives the insured limited discretion over the separate account. See also *equity linked; indexed life; life insurance; whole life insurance.*

variable premium life a form of whole life insurance in which the policyowner determines the amount of premium that will be paid. This amount is subject to minimum and maximum range requirements spelled out in the policy. As the premium level varies, so will the cash value and death benefit. See also *flexible premium life; life insurance; premium; universal life; whole life insurance.*

vesting the right of an employee to the assets contributed in his or her name, to an employer's retirement plan. Contributions are made for new employees from the date of eligibility. However, the employee does not acquire ownership of those contributions until vesting reaches 100%. This is an incentive to employees not to terminate employment before the full vesting date.

Under provisions of the Tax Reform Act of 1986, there are two acceptable formulas for the maximum time allowed until full vesting. First is full vesting, in which the employee receives 100% ownership of contributions five years after the eligibility date. Second is 20% vesting per year, beginning after the third year of eligibility, and reaching 100% after the seventh year. See also *Employee Retirement Income Security Act (ERISA); full vesting; immediate vesting; qualified plan; retirement plan; Tax Reform Act of 1986.*

Veterans Group Life Insurance (VGLI) a program offered by the U.S. government to veterans of the armed forces. Upon discharge, SEGLI coverage may be converted to VGLI, providing five-year renewable term life insurance. The policy can be converted to other plans of insurance offered by participating commercial insurance companies, who provide coverage in VGLI on a sharing arrangement. See also *convertible term; government life insurance; group life; life insurance; term life.*

Veterans Group Life Insurance (VGLI)

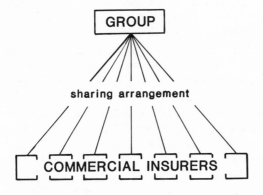

---

void contract a contract that cannot exist under the law. If one of the parties is not legally competent to enter a contract, if the contract contains privileges in violation of the law, if there is no consideration, or if there is no meeting of the minds, the contract is said to never have existed. See also *contract; valid contract.*

voidable contract a contract that can be voided or kept in force, at the option of one of the parties. Example: The insurance company may cancel a contract if it discovers misrepresentation or fraud in an application. Example: A minor who enters a contract of a certain type may, at his or her option, declare the contract void. See also *contract; valid contract.*

voluntary reserve a reserve established by an insurer, beyond statutory requirements. See also *reserve.*

W

wagering the creation of a risk. In comparison to insurance, a wager is a voluntary entry into a risk situation. Insurance is intended as protection against risks that already exist, and when the insured desires protection against resulting economic consequences of loss.

The distinction is an important one in determining insurable interest. For example, the members of a family have such an interest in the life and health of their sole supporter. And a business owner has an insurable interest in property that is insured under a liability and casualty policy.

An individual who applies for insurance who lacks insurable interest is creating a wager, which is not permitted by regulation. For example, an individual offers to purchase an insurance policy and pay the premiums on the life of a friend. Because the person making the offer does not have an insurable interest, this situation would be a wager. The individual would benefit in the event the insured person died. However, the purpose is not to compensate for an untimely loss.

In the event of business property, an individual who does not own that property, or who does not have a collateral interest in it, lacks insurable interest. For example, a business owner has pledged assets as security on a loan. As soon as this occurs, the lender has an insurable interest, and may be named as beneficiary in an insurance policy.

Risks and wagers are further distinguished by the type of loss. A property loss is unlikely but possible. Thus, in the event of a catastrophic loss, an individual with an insurable interest would stand to (a) lose the value of property and be unable to replace it, or (b) lose the security on a collateral arrangement, and become exposed to the risk of default.

Life insurance covers a different type of loss. Death will occur as a certainty. However, the time of death cannot be known in advance. Thus, life insurance protects beneficiaries against premature and unexpected death. Such a death would create economic hardships, and the death benefit is intended to offset or mitigate those hardships.

A wager, by its nature, is not protection or a form of reimbursement. The risk itself arises from the wager, and not from circumstances and exposure beyond the control of the individual. See also *catastrophic loss; insurable interest; risk.*

waiting period (1) a period of time specified in a health insurance policy, during which specified risks are not covered. For example, an individual applies for coverage, and discloses on the application that, six months prior, he underwent surgery on his knee. The insurance company issues the policy with the stipulation that, for a period of three years, any expenses arising from knee problems are excluded from coverage. This pre-existing condition is made subject to a waiting period.

(2) the number of days or months that an employee is excluded from participation in a group insurance policy. For example, an employee is hired on January 1. Under the terms of a group health insurance policy, there is a one-month waiting period before coverage takes effect.

See also *elimination period; health insurance; pre-existing condition; probationary period.*

waiver a clause in a policy, or an agreement attached to the policy, that excludes specific losses from coverage.

Example: An applicant for health insurance has a history of heart problems. The insurer issues the policy with a waiver, stating that expenses incurred due to heart problems are excluded from coverage.

Example: A property and casualty policy is issued to the owner of a manufacturing company, which stores hazardous materials at its premises. The policy includes a waiver stating that no coverage is provided for losses arising from damages or injury caused by those materials.

See also *exclusion; loss prevention.*

Waiver of Premium (WP) a benefit in certain policies, stating that under some conditions, coverage will continue in force without the requirement for continuation of premium payments. For example, a disability policy includes a WP provision, stating that while disabled and receiving benefits, the insured is excused from making premium payments. Upon conclusion of the disability, the premiums must be resumed in order for the policy to remain in force. See also *disability benefit; rider.*

Welfare and Pension Plans Disclosure Act (WPPDA)   a federal law stating filing requirements for administrators of certain pension plans. Each plan with 25 or more participants must file a plan description with the Department of Labor, including a copy of the plan itself, form of administration, and benefits. For plans in which 100 or more people are eligible for benefits, yearly financial statements are an added requirement. See also *pension plan*.

whole life annuity   an annuity in which benefit payments will continue for the remainder of the annuitant's life. See also *annuity*.

whole life insurance   a plan of life insurance that combines protection and a growing cash value, or savings element. As the amount of cash value increases, the insurance decreases. Eventually, the entire face value will represent cash value, and no insurance will remain. Policies are designed to achieve 100% cash value in a specified number of years or by a specific age.

Policyowners are allowed to borrow their cash value for any purpose. If loans are not repaid, the face amount of the policy is reduced. The value that builds in the policy cannot be lost. Upon surrender, the full cash value must be paid, or applied in other optional settlement modes of the insured's choosing. See also *cash value; ordinary life; policy loan; savings element; surrender value*.

whole life insurance

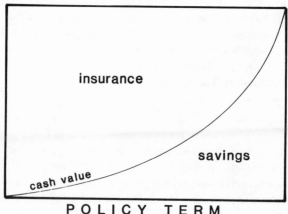

POLICY TERM

wholesale life   a form of life insurance similar to group insurance, but in which each participant receives an individual policy.

A group life insurance contract is owned by the employer or other head of a group, whereas a wholesale life policy is owned by the participant. The terms and provisions of each wholesale life policy are identical for all covered individuals. See also *group life; life insurance.*

---

wholesale life

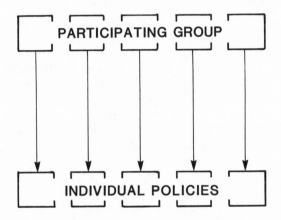

---

will   documentation of the wishes of a deceased person regarding distribution of property. Excluded from a testamentary estate are properties held in joint tenancy registration, life insurance in which a living beneficiary is named, and property in a living trust. See also *estate planning.*

Women Leaders Round Table (WLRT)   an association created by the National Association of Life Underwriters (NALU), that recognizes women life insurance agents who meet annual volume requirements. See also *agent; life insurance; National Association of Life Underwriters (NALU).*

workers compensation   a form of insurance that, by state law, every employer must provide to employees. It provides compensation for losses arising from medical expenses, disability and liability for work-related injuries and accidents. See also *disability; employee; health insurance.*

worldwide coverage   expanded business liability coverage that provides for reimbursement of losses occurring in foreign countries. Some forms of worldwide coverage limit the amount of liability protection offered overseas. See also *business liability; Comprehensive General Liability (CGL); liability insurance.*

written business   paid business, those policies in which applications have been signed and initial premiums received, but which have not yet been approved by the company's underwriter. See also *in force; new business.*

written premium   money received for modal premium payments, which may be earned or unearned. If the policy has not yet been approved, written premium is unearned. Once approved, only the portion of a modal premium related to the current period is earned; the balance is considered unearned, and will remain so until a subsequent period. Example: the first premium annual is paid with submission of an application on December 10. However, the underwriting process is not completed until the end of the month, and the policy is issued with an anniversary date of January 1. During the period December 10 to December 31, the entire period is unearned. One-twelfth of the annual premium is treated as earned, and the balance is unearned. Each month, one-twelfth of the total is recognized as earned premium. See also *earned premium; premium; unearned premium.* See illustration, page 233.

wrongful death   the taking of a life in such a way that liability for damages is claimed. This can arise from intentional acts (murder or manslaughter, for example), or from negligence (such as drunk driving). Anyone who suffers economically from the wrongful death of an individual may file suit in most states to recover damages. See also *economic value; negligence.*

Y

Yearly Renewable Term (YRT)   a form of term insurance that is renewed each year. The renewal privilege is extended for a limited number of years, commonly five or ten. Some forms allow the policyowner to extend to age 65. Premiums rise with each extension, based on the insured's attained age. See also *attained age; life insurance; renewable term; term life.* See illustration, page 233.

years of service   the number of years an employee has worked for an employer. Years of service are used as the basis for calculating vesting

written premium

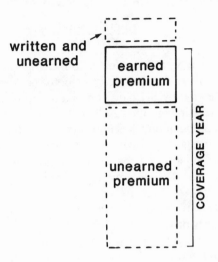

written and
unearned

earned
premium

unearned
premium

COVERAGE YEAR

Yearly Renewable
Term (YRT)

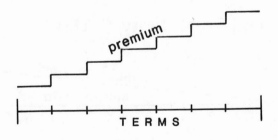

premium

T E R M S

percentage, and also is used in certain benefit formulas. See also *eligible employee; qualified plan; retirement plan; vesting.*

yield on assets   a calculation of the rate of return earned on the basis in assets. For example, a company owns stocks that it bought for $16,000. At the end of one full year, the stock has a market value of $19,000, and the company has received $800 in dividends. By adding together the increase in market value and dividends received ($3,800), and dividing that by the original basis, the yield on assets is computed as 23.75%:

$$\frac{\$3,800 + \$800}{\$16,000} = 23.75\%$$

If assets are held for a period shorter or longer than one year, the yield should be annualized (so that comparisons between assets are valid). Annualization is computed by dividing computed returns by the number of months held, and multiplying the result by 12 (one year).

A more exact computation takes into account the time value of money. Returns earned over a period of years carry greater weight than short-term returns, on the assumption that the original funds were committed for a longer period of time. See also *interest; rate of return; time value of money.*

Yield to Maturity (YTM)   the rate earned on an asset between the date purchased and its maturity date. This is not the same as current yield. For example, an insurance company invests in a bond with five years until maturity date. However, the bond is discounted to a price of 94 (meaning the cost was $940 per $1,000 of maturity value). To compute the YTM, the discount yield must be taken into account, over the period of time until maturity date. See also *discount; interest; maturity value; nominal interest rate; rate of return.*

Yield To Maturity (YTM)

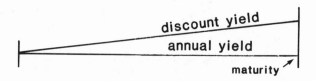

State Insurance
Commissioner Addresses

Commissioner of Insurance
135 South Union Street
Montgomery, Alabama 36130
(205) 269-3550

Director of Insurance
Pouch D
Juneau, Alaska 99811
(907) 465-2515

Director of Insurance
1601 West Jefferson
Phoenix, Arizona 85007
(602) 255-4862

Insurance Commissioner
400-18 University Tower Building
Little Rock, Arkansas 72204
(501) 371-1325

Insurance Commissioner
14th Floor
600 South Commonwealth
Los Angeles, California 90005
(213) 736-2551

Commissioner of Insurance
5th Floor
303 West Colfax
Denver, Colorado 80204
(303) 573-3410

Insurance Commissioner
Room 425
165 Capitol Avenue
Hartford, Connecticut 06106
(203) 566-2810

Insurance Commissioner
21 The Green
Dover, Delaware 19901
(302) 736-4251

Superintendent of Insurance
Suite 512
614 H Street, N.W.
Washington, DC 20001
(202) 727-7419

Insurance Commissioner
Plaza Level 11
State Capitol Building
Tallahassee, Florida 32301
(904) 488-3440

Insurance Commissioner
Suite 716
West Tower Floyd Building
#2 Martin Luther King, Jr. Drive
Atlanta, Georgia 30334
(404) 656-2056

Insurance Commissioner
1010 Richards Street
Honolulu, Hawaii 96813
(808) 548-7505

Director of Insurance
700 West State Street
Boise, Idaho 83720
(208) 334-2250

Director of Insurance
4th Floor
320 West Washington Street
Springfield, Illinois 62701
(217) 782-4515

Commissioner of Insurance
509 State Office Building
Indianapolis, Indiana 46204
(317) 232-2386

Commissioner of Insurance
G23, Ground Floor
State Office Building
Des Moines, Iowa 50319
(515) 281-5705

Commissioner of Insurance
420 Southwest 9th Street
Topeka, Kansas 66612
(913) 296-3071

Insurance Commissioner
229 West Main Street
Frankfort, Kentucky 40602
(502) 564-3630

Commissioner of Insurance
P.O. Box 94214
Baton Rouge, Louisiana 70804
(504) 342-5328

Superintendent of Insurance
Hollowell Annex
Station #34, State House
Augusta, Maine 04333
(207) 289-3101

Insurance Commissioner
7th Floor South
501 St. Paul Place
Baltimore, Maryland 21202
(301) 659-6300

Commissioner of Insurance
100 Cambridge Street
Boston, Massachusetts 02202
(617) 727-3333

Commissioner of Insurance
P.O. Box 30220
Lansing, Michigan 48909
(517) 373-0220

Deputy Commissioner of
  Commerce
5th Floor
500 Metro Square Building
St. Paul, Minnesota 55101
(612) 296-6907

Commissioner of Insurance
1804 Walter Sillers Building
Jackson, Mississippi 39205
(601) 359-3569

Director of Insurance
301 West High, Route 630
Jefferson City, Missouri 65102
(314) 751-2451

Commissioner of Insurance
Mitchell Building
Helena, Montana 59604
(406) 444-2996

Director of Insurance
301 Centennial Mall South
State Office Building
Lincoln, Nebraska 68509
(402) 471-2201

Commissioner of Insurance
Nye Building
201 South Falls Street
Carson City, Nevada 89710
(702) 885-4270

Insurance Commissioner
169 Manchester Street
Concord, New Hampshire 03301
(603) 271-2261

Commissioner of Insurance
201 East State Street
Trenton, New Jersey 08625
(609) 292-5363

Superintendent of Insurance
PERA Building
P.O. Drawer 1269
Santa Fe, New Mexico 87504
(505) 827-4535

Superintendent of Insurance
160 West Broadway
New York, New York 10013
(212) 602-0429

Commissioner of Insurance
Dobbs Building
P.O. Box 26387
Raleigh, North Carolina 27611
(919) 733-7343

Commissioner of Insurance
5th Floor
Capitol Building
Bismarck, North Dakota 58505
(701) 224-2444

Director of Insurance
2100 Stella Court
Columbus, Ohio 43215
(614) 466-3584

Insurance Commissioner
408 Will Rogers Memorial
    Building
Oklahoma City, Oklahoma 73105
(405) 521-2828

Insurance Commissioner
Commerce Building
Salem, Oregon 97310
(503) 378-4271

Commissioner of Insurance
13th Floor
Strawberry Square
Harrisburg, Pennsylvania 17120
(717) 787-5173

Commissioner of Insurance
P.O. Box 8330
Fernandez Juntos Station
Santurce, Puerto Rico 00910
(809) 724-6565

Insurance Commissioner
100 North Main Street
Providence, Rhode Island 02903
(401) 277-2223

Insurance Commissioner
2711 Middleburg Drive
Columbia, South Carolina 29204
(803) 758-3266

Director of Insurance
Insurance Building
320 North Nicollet
Pierre, South Dakota 57501
(605) 773-3563

Commissioner of Commerce and
Insurance
114 State Office Building
Nashville, Tennessee 37219
(615) 741-2241

State Board of Insurance
1110 San Jacinto Boulevard
Austin, Texas 78786
(512) 475-3726

Commissioner of Insurance
160 East 300 South
Salt Lake City, Utah 84145
(801) 530-6400

Commissioner of Banking and
Insurance
State Office Building
Montpelier, Vermont 05602
(802) 828-3301

Commissioner of Insurance
700 Jefferson Building
Richmond, Virginia 23209
(804) 786-3741

Commissioner of Insurance
Office of the Lieutenant Governor
P.O. Box 450
Charlotte Amalie
St. Thomas, Virgin Islands 00801
(809) 774-2991

Insurance Commissioner
Insurance Building AQ21
Olympia, Washington 98504
(206) 753-7301

Insurance Commissioner
2100 Washington Street East
Charleston, West Virginia 25305
(304) 348-3386

Commissioner of Insurance
P.O. Box 7873
Madison, Wisconsin 53707
(608) 266-3585

Insurance Commissioner
Herschler Building
122 West 25th Street
Cheyenne, Wyoming 82002
(307) 777-7401

Canadian Provincial Agency Addresses

Consumer and Corporate Affairs
  Department
1100 Capitol Square
10065 Jasper Avenue
Edmonton, Alberta T5J 3B1
(403) 427-4095

Ministry of Consumer and
  Corporate Affairs
940 Blanshard Street
Victoria, British Columbia
  V8V 1X4
(604) 387-1251

Consumer and Corporate Affairs
  Department
114 Garry Street
Winnipeg, Manitoba R3C 1G1
(204) 956-2040

Consumer Affairs Division
  Justice Department
P.O. Box 6000
Fredericton, New Brunswick
  E3B 5H1
(506) 453-2659

Department of Consumer Affairs
  and Communications
Elizabeth Towers
P.O. Box 4750

St. John's, Newfoundland A1C 5T7
(709) 576-2591

Department of Consumer Affairs
5151 Terminal Road
P.O. Box 998
Halifax, Nova Scotia B3J 2X3
(902) 424-4690

Ministry of Consumer and
  Commercial Relations
555 Yonge Street
Toronto, Ontario M7A 2H6
(416) 963-1111

Consumer Services Division
  Justice Department
P.O. Box 2000
Charlottetown, Prince Edward
  Island C1A 7N8
(902) 892-5411

Ministère de la Protection du
  Consommateur
6 rue de L'Université
Québec, P.Q. G1R 5G8
(418) 643-1557

Department of Consumer and
  Commercial Affairs
1871 Smith Street
Regina, Saskatchewan S4P 3V7
(306) 787-5550

Abbreviations

AAA	American Academy of Actuaries
AALU	Association for Advanced Life Underwriting
AC	American College
ACLI	American Council of Life Insurance
ACV	Actual Cash Value
AIA	American Insurance Association
AIPLU	American Institute for Property and Liability Underwriters
ANC	Average Net Cost
ARIA	American Risk and Insurance Association
ASCLU	American Society of Chartered Life Underwriters
ASO	Administrative Services Only
ASV	Asset Share Value
BAP	Business Automobile Policy
BOP	Business Owner's Policy
CAS	Casualty Actuarial Society
CCIA	Consumer Credit Insurance Association
CEBS	Certified Employee Benefit Specialist
CFA	Chartered Financial Analyst
CFP	Certified Financial Planner
CGL	Comprehensive General Liability
ChFC	Chartered Financial Consultant
CLU	Chartered Life Underwriter
COB	Coordination of Benefits
COLA	Cost of Living Adjustment
CPCU	Chartered Property and Casualty Underwriter
CSI	Commissioners Standard Industrial Mortality Table
CSO	Commissioners Standard Ordinary Mortality Table
DITC	Disability Insurance Training Council
DOC	Drive Other Car endorsement
ERISA	Employee Retirement Income Security Act
ESOP	Employee Stock Ownership Plan
ESOT	Employee Stock Ownership Trust

FAIR	Fair Access to Insurance Requirements
FCAS	Fellow, Casualty Actuarial Society
FCRA	Fair Credit Reporting Act
FDIC	Federal Deposit Insurance Corporation
FEGLI	Federal Employees Group Life Insurance
FELA	Federal Employees Liability Act
FHA	Federal Housing Administration
FIA	Federal Insurance Administration
FIA	Fellow, Institute of Actuaries
FICA	Federal Insurance Contributions Act
FLMI	Fellow, Life Management Institute
FMDF	Five Million Dollar Forum
FPA	Free of Particular Average
FSA	Federal Security Agency
FSA	Fellow, Society of Actuaries
FSLIC	Federal Savings and Loan Insurance Corporation
FTC	Federal Trade Commission
GA	General Agent
GAAP	Generally Accepted Accounting Principles
GAB	General Adjustment Bureau
GAMC	General Agents and Managers Conference
HIAA	Health Insurance Association of America
HII	Health Insurance Institute
HMO	Health Maintenance Organization
HOLUA	Home Office Life Underwriters Association
IAC	Interest Adjusted Cost
IAHU	International Association of Health Underwriters
IASA	Insurance Accounting and Statistical Association
IBNR	Incurred But Not Reported
ICA	International Claim Association
IESA	Insurance Economic Society of America
IIA	Insurance Institute of America
IIAA	Independent Insurance Agents of America
III	Insurance Information Institute
ILCM	Individual Level Cost Method
ILI	Institute of Life Insurance
ILR	Incurred Loss Ratio
IMUA	Inland Marine Underwriters Association
IRA	Individual Retirement Account
IRA	Individual Retirement Annuity
IRIS	Insurance Regulatory Information System
ISAA	Insurance Service Association of America
ISO	Insurance Services Office

JTWROS	Joint Tenancy With Rights of Survivorship
LFM	Loss Frequency Method
LIAA	Life Insurance Association of America
LIC	Life Insurers Conference
LIMRA	Life Insurance Marketing and Research Association
LMI	Life Management Institute
LOMA	Life Office Management Association
LPRT	Leading Producers Round Table
LR	Lapse Ratio
LRRM	Loss Ratio Reserve Method
LUA	Life Underwriters Association
LUTC	Life Underwriters Training Council
MARM	Moving Average Rating Method
MDO	Monthly Debit Ordinary
MDRT	Million Dollar Round Table
MET	Multiple Employer Trust
MFL	Maximum Foreseeable Loss
MIB	Medical Information Bureau
MPL	Maximum Probable Loss
MSVR	Mandatory Securities Valuation Reserve
NAIA	National Association of Insurance Agents
NAIB	National Association of Insurance Brokers
NAIC	National Association of Insurance Commissioners
NAIIA	National Association of Independent Insurance Adjusters
NALC	National Association of Life Companies
NALU	National Association of Life Underwriters
NCCI	National Council on Compensation Insurance
NFIA	National Flood Insurers Association
NFIP	National Flood Insurance Program
NIA	National Insurance Association
NIDC	National Insurance Development Corporation
NIPC	National Insurance Producers Conference
NLP	Net Level Premium
NSLI	National Service Life Insurance
NRS	Numerical Rating System
OASDHI	Old Age, Survivors, Disability, and Health Insurance
OSHA	Occupational Safety and Health Act
OSHA	Occupational Safety and Health Administration
PAP	Personal Automobile Policy
PAYSOP	Payroll Stock Ownership Plan
PBGC	Payroll Benefit Guaranty Corporation
PIA	Primary Insurance Amount
PPGA	Personal Producing General Agent

PPO	Preferred Provider Organization
PPRM	Pure Premium Rating Method
RAM	Reverse Annuity Mortgage
RIMS	Risk and Insurance Management Society
RM	Retrospective Method
RRM	Rate of Return Method
SA	Society of Actuaries
SAA	Surety Association of America
SBLI	Savings Bank Life Insurance
SCPCU	Society of Chartered Property and Casualty Underwriters
SEP	Simplified Employee Pension plan
SGLI	Servicemen's Group Life Insurance
SIPC	Securities Investor Protection Corporation
SIR	Self-Insured Retention
SMI	Special Multiperil Insurance
TDA	Tax-Deferred Annuity
TEFRA	Tax Equity and Fiscal Responsibility Act of 1982
TFCM	Three Factor Contribution Method
TSA	Tax-Sheltered Annuity
UCR	Usual, Customary and Reasonable
UGMA	Uniform Gift to Minors Act
UIASPPA	Uniform Individual Accident and Sickness Policy Provisions Act
URLA	Uniform Reciprocal Licensing Act
USDA	Uniform Simultanous Death Act
USGLI	United States Government Life Insurance
VGLI	Veterans Group Life Insurance
WLRT	Women Leaders Round Table
WP	Waiver of Premium
WPPDA	Welfare and Pension Plans Disclosure Act
YRT	Yearly Renewable Term
YTM	Yield to Maturity